WHY THE HOME CRUMBLES

Biblical Principles to Succeed in Building a Godly Home

Dr. RICHARD JACOB

Copyright © 2010 by Dr. Richard Jacob

Why The Home Crumbles
Biblical Principles to Succeed in Building a Godly Home
by Dr. Richard Jacob

Printed in the United States of America

ISBN 9781609578114

All rights reserved solely by the author. The author guarantees all contents are original and do not infringe upon the legal rights of any other person or work. No part of this book may be reproduced in any form without the permission of the author. The views expressed in this book are not necessarily those of the publisher.

Unless otherwise indicated, Bible quotations are taken from The King James Version (The Ryrie Study Bible). Copyright © 1976 by Moody Press Chicago.

www.xulonpress.com

DEDICATION

THIS BOOK IS DEDICATED TO

MY PRECIOUS LORD AND SAVIOR JESUS CHRIST

And

My Dear Wife Leah

MY SINCERE GRATITUDE

To my sweet wife Leah, my faithful wife and best friend
For her help, patience, love, sacrifice and encouragement
For her godly example

To my three wonderful children Gideon, Emerald and Marcus
For their prayer and love

To Mrs. Veena Jacob (sister-in-law) for her help in editing the book
To my brother Kenneth Jacob for his help and encouragement

To Ms. Gallion for her help in editing the book

TABLE OF CONTENTS

I. I had a dream 15

II. The master plan 28

III. A mighty fortress 44

IV. Rock solid foundation 61

V. Raising strong pillars: Remaining in God's principles 80

VI. Weathering storms 104

VII. Caution!!! What are we building? What are we leaving behind? 136

VIII. The little foxes 172

IX. Except the Lord build the home 206

X.   I couldn't have done it without Him 241

XI. As for me and my house 258

PREFACE

Why does the home crumble? A very good question indeed! I believe the home crumbles because of many reasons. One prime reason could be that most people invest too much time, energy, work, and labor trying to chase after the dream of owning, building or renovating a home. In sharp contrast, very little attention is ever paid to the building of a home.

In a fast paced world, where one is always on the move, time is a priceless commodity. Everyone, everywhere is in a mad rush, trying to juggle so many tasks, trying to squeeze in as much as can be done in a day's time. Don't get me wrong. I am not against anyone owning a house. I am concerned however, about the dream most people chase after. Do their dreams come true? Have they reached their goals? If so, then, at what cost?

While pursuing the dream to own or build a home, one must not fail to consider all that is at stake. What does it cost apart from money? I once heard of a story of a man that loved a woman dearly. He married her. He was willing to make any sacrifice to make her happy. He purposed in his heart to make her the queen of his house. He didn't care how much money it cost him. Thus, he set out on this great adventure to build her a dream house. He kept this project a secret, with the hope of giving her a big surprise. He hired the cream of architects and the best builders. He invested a great deal of money to purchase a dream location. The location he purchased was ideally situated on a little hill near the sea. The scenes were breathtaking.

He envisioned how happy his wife would be when the project was all-complete. Each day, he left home early. He returned home very late, tired and exhausted of all his energies. This dream consumed him. One day, his wife was tired of this. She approached him saying, "I miss you around, honey." She continued, "You are gone all day and I am lonely." To this he replied, "Darling, I'm very busy, there's so much to do." Her complaints grew. He pretended he didn't hear her, for he thought, "When she finally finds out what I am doing, she would be so thrilled." It is for her that he is going through all this pain.

The project took too much time. He made changes to the building trying earnestly to make everything that looked good, look best. This meant building, tearing down, fixing to perfection. Finally, One day his wife reached her wits end, so, packed her bags and left. Incidentally, it was the very day the home had been completed. Upon reaching home, he called out to her in an excited tone of voice. "Honey, I'm home." I won't be late anymore." There was no response. His voice echoed in the death like silence that pursued. Excitement turned to despair. He wanted to show his princess her castle, he had so painstakingly built for her, and her alone. "He phoned her many times, coaxing her to return but his effort was in vain. Going back to his picturesque home, he stood all alone at the door. His palatial home stood elegantly, but there was no princess to complete its beauty and purpose. Many homes will be broken in the pursuit of chasing a dream. Much like this man's dream, it may be a valiant dream, or even a purposeful goal of life. Before you venture to fulfill your dream, ask yourself, "Is it really worth my investment, my time, my energy?" I wonder!

A very sad story indeed! Much is at stake when we chase after a dream. It may be a great dream, but one must count the cost? Is it worthwhile? Jesus taught the value of evaluating the cost of a project before you venture out to actually build it. In Luke 14:28, He said, "For which of you, intending to build a tower, sitteth not down first, and counteth the cost, whether he have sufficient to finish it?" I urge you to count the cost. Count every penny, nickel, dime, dollar, husband, wife, child, time and energy it will cost you, before you invest into something so large. As for me, I'd love to have a house if God provided me one, but I'd rather build a home. How about you? Life is too fleeting for me to squander my time or energy building a house. I'd rather build my home. Think about this, after all we have invested into building a house; can you even take a penny or a piece of furniture or a priced possession to the other side of life? Relationships matter. Friendship counts. The home matters. For this reason, the creation story in Genesis tells of God's desire to make a man and a woman, join them in marriage, to raise a home. He did not build a house. However, He did establish the home. What will you build? Think about it. It will be your decision, yours alone.

CHAPTER ONE

I HAD A DREAM

The sound of horses running, the chirping of birds, the pitter patter of the raindrops on the ceiling, the meandering of the rivers through the forest, the beautiful colors of the flowers, the overgrown bushes, the creepy noises in the dark woods appeal to the senses. The thundering of the waterfall, the touch of a falling leaf, the squeaks of a cracking branch, runs a cold current through one's spine. Fear raises the hair on your back. A gleam of hope like a silver line in a dark cloud appears when a narrow path seems to emerge and lead somewhere. The path is rough, the road is rugged, but there is a silver lining allowing a blue sky to peep through the thicket.

A fresh scent sweeps through the air. Up ahead in the distance there are mountains. Each upward step captivates the eye with the ever-unfolding scene. As if from nowhere, suddenly appear, the pinnacles of a building. It looks magnificent. Is it a palace? Is it a fort? It is so enchanting. Oh! No! It's not a palace, nor is it a fort. It is a Castle! The story begins.

Stories and fairy tales fascinate everyone. Until recent times, stories came alive when fathers and mothers read them from storybooks or when grandparents made up a concoction. The drama begins when the storyteller can mesmerize his audience to live in the moment of his fairy tale. In the modern arena of story telling, there is the amazing animation by Walt Disney that gives story telling a new dimension. Stories live on in dreams. Dreams aren't real all the time but everyone can dream. I, too, had a dream.

As a little boy, I dreamed of things that probably never existed in a real world. Things such as Star wars, Superman, Spiderman and Phantom were real to me. I wondered where all of this existed, if so, was it real. I did not understand or comprehend the difference between, the good, the bad or the ugly. It was all fiction, only wishful thinking. Many other fantasies lurked in my small mind.

In my teenage years, those dreams changed. I dreamed of what I would become. Was I going to be a doctor, an engineer, an inventor, or an archeologist? Thoughts of traveling, to places like Egypt to explore the great pyramids or to Bible lands to excavate the buried cities, all seemed a great possibility. It was the age where I could dare to dream and dream to dare.

As a young adult, my dreams broadened their horizons. I dreamed of whom I would marry. Who would this beautiful princess be? Will she be tall? Where would I find her? Would any girl dare to marry me? I wondered if I would have a family. How many children would

I have? For some unknown reason, I thought at that time, "seven" was some kind of magically perfect number.

I dreamed of the home I might have in the distant future. Where will I build it? What would it look like? Would I be able to really build a castle? All of these things were only dreams. If dreams remain dreams, they live on only to be a fantasy. However, if dreams translate to reality, then dreams live on in actuality. Is it possible for dreams to come true? I really wonder.

DO DREAMS REALLY COME TRUE?

One wonders, do dreams really come true?

   Upon leaving school in 1889, at age sixteen, Andrews began work as a premium apprentice at Harland & Wolff Ltd. shipbuilders in Queen's Island, Belfast. The apprenticeship he served was designed for one intended to end up quite high in the company. He began with three months in the joiner's shop, followed by a month in the cabinetmaker's ship and two months actually working on the ships. Next he spent two months in the main store (warehouse), five months with the shipwrights, two in the moulding loft, two with the painters, eight with the iron shipwrights, six with the fitters, three with the patternmakers, and eight with the smiths. The last eighteen months of his five year term were spent in the drawing office. His great talent for mechanical engineering and construction and his growing leadership abilities singled him out for a bright future, possibly as a senior manager."[1]

Thomas Andrews, "builder of the ship of dreams," was an incredible young man. He made great strides in his endeavor to be a great ship builder. He had some big dreams. He began to turn them into reality, reaching one milestone at a time, keeping in mind, the possibility of making his dream come true. "Andrews became a member of the Institution of Naval Architects in 1901. After working up through several departments, he became the firm's managing director and head of the draughting department."[2]

To get a grip of the extent of the dream of this incredible man, one must study some of the statistics of the great Titanic: It's length (882.75 feet); width (92.5 feet), height (175 feet); weight (46,000 tons); crew (860); and passengers (2, 500). Some more amazing facts include: the number of rivets used (3,000,000); date its keel was laid (31st March 1909) date it was launched (31st May 1911) and the cost to build it (1,500,000 pounds).[3] Truly astounding! Compare this to the building of a home, **not a house**. The Titanic took a lot of planning and building before it was set to sail on her maiden voyage. "The keel for Titanic was laid in March 1909, and her hull was launched May, 1911. She was then towed to a fitting out basin where her interiors were installed. She was completed in Feb 1912. So it basically took 3 years to build the Titanic."[4]

It took a great amount of time to plan how to build the Titanic. Many laborious hours were invested into its layout and design. More than a million and half pounds were lavished on it, to bring this vessel to its fruition. Thomas Andrews and his team envisioned it. The dream was born in the heart and head of one man. It was his dream. He endeavored to build it with a deep passion. However, it would not last forever. In its final moments, before it sank to the bottom of the ocean, on fourteenth of April, "Andrews remarked to a friend that *Titanic* was "as nearly perfect as human brains can make her."[5] Yet, human perfection does not guarantee permanence. Nothing earthly or material is of any eternal value. Everything earthly is temporal in nature. Earthly things are restricted by the boundaries of time, even subject to decay. The human heart craves material things. Thus, in its epicenter there lies the desire to build a home. However, I must ask you a series of probing questions. What are you passionate about in life? You may be busy doing many things, things that may be of great value. But, the most important passion an individual should be concerned about is, the building of one's home, not a house. May I ask, "What are you building?"

WHAT ARE WE BUILDING?

Thousands of people are trying to buy their dream house. They work hard to make a decent living. Most people measure success by material prosperity. They believe in accumulating a big bank balance, building or buying their dream house, but how many truly dream of making a home? Tragically, most Americans of this generation choose the former path. People the world over follow suit. Noelle Knox writes about the trend that is making waves in

America. I quote these paragraphs from *USA TODAY*, "I just got tired of waiting for Mr. Right to come along and start the American dream," says Phelan, who owns her own company, which resells time-shares. Last year, she sold that house and bought a larger one in a gated golf-course community in Reno.

> "They're kind of like emotional trophies," says Phelan, 43. "It's symbolic of success - of getting out there and doing it on my own and saying, 'I'm just as capable of doing it as the next person and doing it on my own and making it.' "
> A lot of other women seem to feel the same way. Last year, single women snapped up one of every five homes sold. That's nearly 1.5 million, if you're counting — more than twice as many as single men bought, according to the National Association of Realtors.[6]

Satan has been successful in distancing man from the Scriptures. Marriage has lost its centrality in modern society. It has lost its sanctity. Families have lost their priority. The term "family" is taken lightly these days. Looks like Satan is winning this battle. Women do not want to get married until late in life. Most men chose the same path. Children are thought of as, "a big burden." Raising them, too arduous a task.

Women desire to maintain their independence. Selfishness reigns supreme. Selfishness and unbelief are the two original sins. These sins are the root cause of unbiblical homes. Painful as it may be, man is drifting from Biblical principles. Believers are slowly slipping away from the sure foundations of the Word of God. Noelle Knows sheds more light on this topic, of pursuing the dream of buying a house. He says:

> The trend is striking, because in 1981, the number of single women and single men home buyers was virtually the same. Since then, the percentage of buyers who are single women has almost doubled, while the percentage of single men buyers slipped 1 percentage point to 9% last year.
>
> This rise of single-women homeowner is part of a greater social and economic shift that is reshaping American life. For the first time in history, women have access to the same resources men have always had – money, social status, power, says Donald Hantula, professor of organizational psychology at Temple University in Philadelphia.
>
> "Women can go and acquire them on their own rather than searching for a mate to provide them. These demographic and social changes are not in line with how we adapted in the hunter-gatherer era."

This trend has been a major culprit in shifting the Biblical focus of a home. Acquiring a house has become a greater goal than building a home. This ideology has become an epidemic. For this reason, marriage has taken the back seat. Notice how true this fact is in this startling statistic:

> **Women (and men) are marrying later.** On average, women now wait until they're nearly 26 to walk down the aisle, about six years later than in 1960, according to Census data. On average, men today marry at age 27, an increase of five years in that same period.
>
> **Divorce:** A Census study showed that 73% of women who married between 1980 and 1984 reached their 10th anniversary, compared with 90% of women who married

between 1945 and 1949. Still, as many as half of all new marriages end in divorce.[8]

Staying married or divorcing one's partner is a decision, oft determined by financial or material gain. Children too, are weighed on the same scale. Most married couples debate the idea of having children, since they care more about making all their payment towards a: mortgage, car, boat, vacation, etc. The list goes on. They think having kids can wait until later.

Satan has convinced men of the following lies: children are a burden; they rob you of your youthfulness; your looks; your time, and even your money. They are too big an investment. They are a burden, not a blessing. Satan makes people believe another lie. He makes us believe the fallacy that children rob one's freedom. Believers fall into his trap. Rather than drawing to and from the principles of the Word of God, they have deviated from it. Many are being sucked into a modern ideological whirlpool.

Is building a home too much to ask for? Is this something God designed? Is it too much of an investment? Is it too big a dream to chase? Is it a dream worthwhile pursuing? Are the stakes too high? Why are men and women afraid of building a HOME? Numerous queries lurk around concerning this issue, but most importantly, answers need to be found.

HOW MUCH ARE YOU WILLING TO INVEST?

My curiosity to find out how much people invest into a buying a house, led me to another individual engaged in a similar quest. An internet article documents the following words by this man:

> I was curious to find out what is currently the most expensive house in the world. Turns out, you would only need to buy a house for more than 70 million pounds to be the owner of the most expensive house in the world. That's not too bad, aye? Pocket change as far as I'm concerned. However, I've checked through various sources and apparently 2 houses in the UK sold for a rumoured 70 million pounds, so I guess there are 2 houses that can be considered the most expensive house in the world.[9]

This magnificent house is located 25 miles outside of London. The neighbors that surround it include the Duchess of York, Elton John. It is close to the Windsor Castle, and the Queen. This house has:

- 103 rooms
- Five swimming pools
- 50-seat screening room
- 24-carat-gold leafing flooring
- Squash court
- Bowling alley
- All-weather, floodlit tennis courts
- 58-acre estate

- 22 bedroom and bathroom suites
- Gate lodge
- Estate manager's office
- Private cinema
- Stables
- Heated marble driveway
- Underground garaging for eight limousines
- A shooting gallery
- 30 self-contained luxury apartments[10]

Hold your horses. This is not the end. CNBC's reports this shocker. It will make you almost jump out of your skin. It reads:

> Russian billionaire Roman Abramovich has reportedly just bought <u>the world's most expensive house</u>. The 41-year-old oil mogul has—according to The National Post—put down, gulp, $500 million for a home in the French Riviera. A half Billion Dollars for a house.
> The home is called La Leopolda, apparently built by Belgium's King Leopold for his mistresses, but past owners include Bill Gates (wow, that's kind of going from one extreme to another—love lair to, well, Bill Gates' house). Abramovich also owns a $30 million home nearby. La Leopolda sits on ten acres and has the best views in Southern France. The Russian, who also owns the Chelsea Football Club, reportedly decided to buy the house after a private tour he took with his 25-year-old girlfriend.[11]

Why The Home Crumbles

I wonder, how much will you invest in buying or building your dream house? Is this your life's ambition? Are you going to spend all of your time and money chasing after this dream? I urge you to ponder a much bigger question. Search your heart and mind before you juggle up an answer. Are you going to invest every iota of your breath trying to build a HOUSE? Alternatively, are you going to put your life's blood into building a HOME? This is a choice every individual must make for himself.

In my early childhood years, I heard someone make a statement. I heard it many times thereafter. I later saw these words engraved on wall plaques. They read, "There is no place like home." What a simple, yet profound phrase this is. It has captivated my dream, so I choose to pass it on with as much emphasis and redundancy as possible. John Payne's poem asserts to the validity of this statement:

Home Sweet Home

> Mid pleasures and palaces though we may roam,
> Be it ever so humble, there's no place like home;
> A charm from the sky seems to hallow us there,
> Which, seek through the world, is ne'er met with elsewhere.
> Home, home, sweet, sweet home!
> There's no place like home, oh, there's no place like home!
>
> An exile from home, splendor dazzles in vain;
> Oh, give me my lowly thatched cottage again!
> The birds singing gayly, that come at my call-

Give me them — and the peace of mind, dearer than all!
Home, home, sweet, sweet home!
There's no place like home, oh, there's no place like home!

I gaze on the moon as I tread the drear wild,
And feel that my mother now thinks of her child,
As she looks on that moon from our own cottage door
Thro' the woodbine, whose fragrance shall cheer me no more.
Home, home, sweet, sweet home!
There's no place like home, oh, there's no place like home!

How sweet 'tis to sit 'neath a fond father's smile,
And the caress of a mother to soothe and beguile!
Let others delight mid new pleasures to roam,
But give me, oh, give me, the pleasures of home.
Home, home, sweet, sweet home!
There's no place like home, oh, there's no place like home!

To thee I'll return, overburdened with care;
The heart's dearest solace will smile on me there;
No more from that cottage again will I roam;
Be it ever so humble, there's no place like home.
Home, home, sweet, sweet, home!
There's no place like home, oh, there's no place like home![12]

A wonderful poem indeed! What an incredible dream to dream. Nothings compares to the joy of belonging in a home. A home makes you feel: safe; provides unconditional love and security. A home provides warmth. Here one experiences care. It is a place where loved ones shelter you from emotional, mental, and other storms as well. I dared to dream and dream I did. However, to live in a dream world alone will do no good. I quote J.M Power's words to affirm what I am trying to communicate. He says, "If you want to make your dreams come true, the first thing you have to do is wake up."[13] I would like to add a phrase to this quote in conclusion to this chapter, "If you want to make your dreams come true, the first thing you have to do is wake up", wake up to the Word of God, the teachings of the Holy Scriptures, the Bible.

The Bible discloses the enormity of its significance in a person's life. Psalm 119: 105 reads, "Thy word is a lamp unto my feet, and a light unto my path." The Bible is God's Word. It reveals God's mind. The Bible is Gods guide, our compass. It is the map. It has the blue print to help us build a home. It can help us build a sure home. *MAN CAN ONLY BUILD A HOUSE AT BEST (Temporal), BUT ONLY GOD CAN BUILD A HOME.*

CHAPTER TWO

THE MASTER PLAN

A proper building cannot be constructed without first drawing a proper plan. The first step towards constructing a building is to draw a blue print. This gives the edifice a face, if you will. It helps one see what the finished product will look like. Engineers painstakingly produce a blue print. This becomes the builder's guide. The plan or blue print contains all the necessary specifications. Following it meticulously, ensures the builder of accomplishing the architect's desired end.

Modern technology allows architects to see in or around a house or building before a single stone is laid. They can take a sneak-peek in at every nook and corner with the use of computers. Three dimensional computer images produce a realistic image. This capability allows one to see how the house will look when completed. It enables us to view the house from every possible angle. Computer graphics, allows one to view the arrangements of furniture, color of paint on a wall, interior decoration and even external landscaping.

Changes to any one aspect or more, is possible just by the click of a button or the twitch of the mouse. To illustrate this fact, one needs only look back to a recent event that was the limelight of the whole world. The Olympic Games had all its main events take place in the spectacular Beijing Olympic stadium. Such a stunning building just did not appear from nowhere. It has a history. It began with the plan.

>Herzog and DeMeuron's Olympic Stadium, fondly referred to by some as the "Bird's Nest," is a feat of engineering, an aesthetic marvel, and an uber-green machine to boot. What we love most about the stadium's design is its integration of a myriad complex systems all rolled into such an aesthetically and conceptually simple and stunning object. The Swiss architects describe it best, saying, "The spatial effect of the stadium is novel and radical and yet simple and of an almost archaic immediacy. Its appearance is pure structure. Facade and structure are identical."[1]

This breathtaking building has a story behind it. Before we look into the plan and design aspect of this story, let us catch a glimpse of some of its startling statistics.

Full name:	National Stadium
Location:	Beijing, China
Broke ground:	24 December, 2003
Opened:	28 June, 2008
Surface:	Grass

Construction cost:	US$423 million
Architect:	Herzog & de Meuron
Structural engineer:	Arup, China Architectural Design & Research Group
Capacity:	80,000 91,000 (2008 Olympics)[2]

The following intricate details add flavor to this story. Twenty-four trussed columns encase the inner bowl of this incredible stadium with each truss weighing 1,000 tons. It took some 17,000 workers when construction was at its peak. This is the largest steel stadium or structure in the world, using 110,000 tons of steel. The grass field was laid on 14 May 2008. It covered an area of about 7,811 square meters, all of which was laid in 24 hours.

This incredible structure first began with an investment of much energy, time, design and planning. Before a building goes up into construction, many designs are drawn. The best design is chosen. Wikipedia discloses in brevity the choosing of the winning design over all of its contenders.

> The design was awarded to a submission from the Swiss architecture firm Herzog & de Meuron in April 2003, after a bidding process that included 13 final submissions. The design, which originated from the study of Chinese ceramics, implemented steel beams in order to hide supports

for the retractable roof; giving the stadium the appearance of a "Bird's nest". Ironically, the retractable roof was later removed from the design after inspiring the stadium's most recognizable aspect.[6] Ground was broken in December 2003, and the stadium officially opened in June 2008.³

The Beijing Olympic stadium took more than five years to build. Such a mammoth task could have never been accomplished without a proper plan. It would be impossible to visualize such a gargantuan task without a proper design. It took many laborious hours to plan. Finally the edifice got underway. It cost more than time, money and material. Some workers died in its building process. "At its height, 17,000 construction workers worked on the stadium.[14] In January 2008, The Times reported that 10 workers had died throughout construction; despite denial from the Chinese government.[15] However, in a story the following week, Reuters, with the support of the Chinese government, reported that only two workers had died."⁴ However, precious lives were lost in the erecting of such an astounding monument.

One hundred and ten thousand tons of steel was used to build this stadium, making it the largest steel structure in the world. All the steel had been produced in China. A stadium such as the bird's nest was built to host one major event. It took many years to build. Millions of dollars were spent to bring it to fruition.

How much more planning, time, energy and toil must be put into building a home, if it is to last a lifetime! Building a home is the best investment a human being can ever make. You cannot take a penny to the other side of life, but you can take your family into eternity. Can you? If this is true, then, what essentials must be taken into consideration to ensure that a home is built right? I truly believe a home must be built to last. This is God's idea, not mine. It must be strong. It must capable of withstanding the storms of life. It must stand the test of time. It must have the right ingredients. It should have the best plan, design and formula.

What possibly could be the secret formula? Is there such a formula, one wonders? If God wants us to build a durable home, he has to provide us with that secret formula. In fact, he has given us this secret formula. Read on to find out.

THE DIVINE FORMULA
TAKING THE FIRST STEP IN THE RIGHT DIRECTION

Since man cannot come up with a formula for making a successful home, God alone can provide one for man. The Bible is the written Word of God. In it, God graciously discloses: His plans; His purposes; His design for man; His laws; His principles; His direction and His Divine formula for success in any realm. The Bible is the believer's compass. He must follow it in its entirety in order to succeed. He is not to add to its content, nor take away an iota from it.

No human formula will ensure the home a firm foundation. Notice, the human heart is tainted with sin and man is totally depraved. This makes it impossible for him to come up with a master plan. Any plan he may formulate is bound to fail. Since the fall, man's thinking is warped. His thinking will change only when he chooses to accept God as his Savior. His reasoning will change once he makes amends with God. God clearly states in His word that salvation is not by works. He has done the work for salvation. Jesus died for the sin of all men. He was buried, and then on the third day He rose again, according to the Scriptures. I Corinthians 15:3-4 reads, "For I delivered unto you first of all that which I also received, how that Christ died for our sins according to the scriptures; And that he was buried, and that he rose again the third day according to the scriptures." Man's sin has made him an enemy of God, but God still loves man. He sent his son to die as man's substitute.

Every man may now accept this free-gift of salvation. This is a personal decision.

Every man must do so, individually. The Bible says, (Romans 10: 9) "That if thou shalt confess with thy mouth the Lord Jesus, and shalt believe in thine heart that God hath raised him from the dead, thou shalt be saved." The following verse gives the reason why one must do so. Romans 10:10 says, "For with the heart man believeth unto righteousness; and with the mouth confession is made unto salvation." When man has reconciled with God he has restored his relationship with Him. Do you want to have success in building your home? If so, you must first put your trust in the Lord Jesus Christ. You must believe in Jesus as your personal savior. This is the first step in the right direction towards building a solid home.

Once a person has received Christ as his personal Savior, he has assurance of salvation. Assurance of salvation simply means a saved sinner can never be lost. The saved person cannot lose his salvation because salvation is not based on the sinner's condition but on the savior's completed sacrifice. For a long time, as a new Christian, I struggled with my sin (after salvation). In fact, after I got saved, I did not live the perfect life. I messed up many times. Each time I sinned, I felt I lost my salvation. This made my life miserable. On July 19, 1989, Dr. Franks opened the Bible and shared with me John 10:28-29, putting an end to my misery. I found assurance. Many born again believers have the same problem. For your benefit I would like to quote John 10:28. It reads: "And I give unto them eternal life; and they shall never perish, neither shall any man pluck them out of my hand." God emphasizes his promise of eternal security again in verse 29 by saying, "My Father, which gave them me, is greater than all; and no man is able to pluck them out of my Father's hand." Becoming God's child brings you into a new position. It establishes a new relationship with God. God is now your heavenly Father. A son's relationship with his father may change but His "relationship" (father-son) will never change. This is equally true of God's child.

Salvation changes the sinners stand. He now has a new position in Christ. Changing one's status from "sinner" to "saved" aligns one's thoughts with God. Living the Christian life without Christ is the most futile endeavor. Anything accomplished for Christ that is not in accordance to His Word will fail to account for any rewards in eternity. Notice what Jesus said to the people who professed to have done great things in Christ's name in Matthew 7: 21. This passage of Scripture reads, "Not every one that saith unto me, Lord, Lord, shall enter into the kingdom of heaven; but he that doeth the will of my Father which is in heaven." A mere profession of knowing Christ is self foolery. Knowledge of someone does not mean one has a relationship with that person. In the same reading verse 22 states, "Many will say to me in that day, Lord, Lord, have we not prophesied in thy name? And in thy name have cast out devils? And in thy name done many wonderful works? Notice the shocking response of Jesus in verse 23, "And then will I profess unto them, I never knew you: depart from me, ye that work iniquity." No man can rely upon his mind. No believer should. His dependence has to always be on the Lord.

Salvation has changed the sinner's position but it has not changed our person completely. Changing the person is the process of a lifetime. This is practical sanctification. This change can only take place when we work in conjunction with God. Though the believer now thinks of God, he battles another problem, the sin nature. This battle must be fought on a daily basis. So, what must he do to ensure success? God has given him a manual to follow. In it are penned God's mandates. The Bible is the Word of God. It reveals the mind of God.

Hence, it is the Christian's compass. An unknown author describes the Bible so eloquently well in the following poem,

The Bible

The Bible reveals the mind of God,
The state of man,
The way of salvation,
The doom of sinners,
And the happiness of believers.

Its doctrines are holy,
Its precepts are binding,
Its histories are true,
And its decisions are immutable.
Read it to be wise,
Believe it to be safe,
And practice it to be holy.
It contains light to direct you,
Food to support you,
And comfort to cheer you.

It is the traveler's map,
The pilgrim's staff,
The pilot's compass,
The soldier's sword,
And the Christian's charter.
Here, too, Paradise is restored,
Heaven is opened,
And the gates of Hell disclosed.

The Lord Jesus Christ is its grand subject,
Our good its design,
And the glory of God its end.
Let it fill the memory,

Rule the heart,
And guide the feet.
Read it slowly,
Frequently, prayerfully.
It is a mine of wealth,
A paradise of glory,
And a river of pleasure.
It is given you in life,
Will be opened at the judgement,
And be remembered forever.
It involves the highest responsibilty,
Will reward the greatest labor,
And will condemn all who
Trifle with its sacred contents.

Owned, it is riches;
Studied, it is wisdom;
Trusted, it is salvation;
Lived, it is character;
And obeyed, it is power.[5]

Building a home that lasts is God's desire. God instituted the home. He performed the first wedding. Even before the Tabernacle, the Temple or the Church, God established the home. God spoke the world into existence by His Word. The Bible is His Word. He is the living Word. The Bible is the written Word. You cannot separate the person and the Word that He speaks. Using the Bible will aid us to build the home God wants us to have. Such a home will glorify God. How precarious to build it without God's guidelines. Let us be careful to use it as our plumb line, our measure, our ruler. Using it to guide us will surely help us build a home that stands strong.

THE DIVINE FORMULA FOR SUCCESS

To ensure success in building a home, it is imperative that one must use God's Word, for in it is embedded God's secret formula. The divine formula is disclosed in Romans 11:36, "For of him, and through him, and to him, are all things: to whom be glory for ever. Amen." God's modus operandi for success clearly states the fact; a home can never be built in a triumphant manner if we do not include God. God must be the epicenter of all our doings. We need Him to be actively involved in our life's dreams. He is our key to success. Let us uncover his formula for success.

THE DIVINE TRIANGLE AND THE THREE ESSENTIALS

Romans 11: 36, unearths God's formula concealed in it, the divine triangle. It unravels the secret formula. A triangle is a wonderful design. It provides a solid base. Engineers and architects use shapes in buildings for special reasons. One reason is to provide esthetics. Another reason has to do with the stability a design or shape provides. A building must be functional, strong and stable. Though esthetics provides a building with beauty, beauty alone will not keep it standing for a long period of time. This could be a key reason marriages fail. Partners in marriage are drawn to each other by the outward. The outward does play a vital role in attracting our mates but there's got to be more to it. Looking into an individual's personality is a good place to begin in any relationship.

Getting back to shapes, we find rectangles are commonly used in buildings. This shape is used in our homes for windows, door frames, etc. This is purely a shape used to provide similarity. Similarity provides symmetry and balance. A rectangle is not a very strong shape, hence it is very unstable. Notice what the Teachers Domain has to say concerning shapes,

> If there is a single most important shape in engineering, it is the triangle. Unlike a rectangle, a triangle cannot be deformed without changing the length of one of its sides or breaking one of its joints. In fact, one of the simplest ways to strengthen a rectangle is to add supports that form triangles at the rectangle's corners or across its diagonal length. A single support between two diagonal corners greatly strengthens a rectangle by turning it into two triangles.
>
> Arches are also very strong shapes. A force applied to the top of an arch, for example, will be carried vertically and horizontally in an arc along the length of the arch's sides all the way to its base. Still, very heavy loads can cause an arch to deform, or bend. To overcome this weakness, engineers sometimes strengthen arches with heavy buttresses or walls along their sides and bases. If an arch is rotated 360 degrees in a circle, it becomes a strong, three-dimensional, symmetrical shape — a dome.[6]

God in His infinite wisdom has provided an amazing formula that incorporates the Divine Triangle. The three essentials to this divine formula are plain and simple. Romans 11:36 discloses these three essentials sides to this divine triangle. They are as follows: (1) Of Him, (2) Through Him and (3) To Him.

The only way to build a home to withstand trials is by using God's divine formula. His formula works to build a home that is enduring in nature. Let me explain. A home begins when a man and a woman believe it is the will of God for them to be married. Though God implants the desire for a man to unite with a woman and vice versa, it still has to be a plan that originates with God. Permit me to present the three sides incorporated into the making of a home. First, God must be the initiator of the marriage or in other words, the marriage must be in the will of God. Second, a home must be kept by or through the power of God. A marriage has to be sustained by God's help. Lastly, a home must glorify God. Thus, we can conclusive say it is God who initiates, enables and ensures the success of the home.

God in His infinite wisdom saw it fit to use this divine triangle. He provides us the formula for success. The believer is free to use it to pursue success in any area of life, yet making sure he is doing the will of God. This is especially true in relation to building a home.

The shape of a triangle is so uniquely strong. Hence, it is used in the construction of bridges and structures that are required to take on heavy loads. Triangles are also used to form spheres.

> The Spaceship Earth in Orlando, Florida was designed by Walt Disney World. It was completed in 1982. This geodesic dome was constructed from 1450 steel struts, and each

strut was wrapped with a waterproof neoprene covering. The framework was then covered with a skin of nearly one thousand triangular aluminum panels bolted to the struts. The Spaceship Earth dome was engineered and built to withstand wind speeds up to two hundred miles per hour, because Florida occasionally experiences hurricane-force winds.[7]

The Spaceship Earth is an excellent design, a wonderful example of a design built to take on heavy loads of strength-to-weight ratios. Bridges, monuments and domes use triangles in their framework because they distribute stress evenly to all areas of the structure. Life has many challenges. Life poses many threats to the home. Many difficulties will confront it. Many challenges threaten its foundation and its structure. Hardships, poverty, sickness, gossip, finances, emotions, and desires will all test its strength and its stability. Trials of every kind will try to shake it, rock its very foundations, and threaten its existence.

God in His infinite wisdom saw it fit to provide man with this formula so man can depend on God to build the home. Man cannot find in himself the strength, the temper nor the torsion to withstand the pressures, the bending or breaking points that threaten to destroy the home. He needs God's help. Yet, God will not force any man to use His formula. Man voluntarily must choose God's help. The wise man sees the need to use God's wisdom and guidance. Get God involved in this endeavor. Involve God in your life's valuable project. This is the wisest thing to do.

God is immovable. He is unchanging. This makes Him dependable. He is all-powerful. He is an all-wise God. Seek His counsel. Have Him guide you each step of the way. Making Him part of your plans will reap rich rewards. Your home will stand secure. It will withstand the stresses of daily existence. It will weather the storms of life. God is strong, so is His word. The Bible is unmovable too. His word provides the perfect standards by which to build. A hymn writer Haldor Lillenas pens these beautiful words about the Bible,

The Bible Stands

>The Bible stands like a rock undaunted
>'Mid the raging storms of time;
>Its pages burn with the truth eternal,
>And they glow with a light sublime.
>
>The Bible stands though the hills may tumble,
>It will firmly stand when the earth shall crumble;
>I will plant my feet on its firm foundation,
>For the Bible stands.
>
>The Bible stands like a mountain towering
>Far above the works of men;
>Its truth by none ever was refuted,
>And destroy it they never can.
>
>The Bible stands though the hills may tumble,
>It will firmly stand when the earth shall crumble;
>I will plant my feet on its firm foundation,
>For the Bible stands.

The Bible stands and it will forever,
When the world has passed away;
By inspiration it has been given,
All its precepts I will obey.

The Bible stands though the hills may tumble,
It will firmly stand when the earth shall crumble;
I will plant my feet on its firm foundation,
For the Bible stands.

The Bible stands every test we give it,
For its Author is divine;
By grace alone I expect to live it,
And to prove and to make it mine.

The Bible stands though the hills may tumble,
It will firmly stand when the earth shall crumble;
I will plant my feet on its firm foundation,
For the Bible stands.[8]

Now that we have effectively found the formula for success in the written Word of God, the Bible, we must integrate it at every stage in the building of the home. You can build upon this rock. It is both reliable and most dependable. Its precepts will guide, help, establish, and pave the path to erecting a successful home. Next, we must erect a mighty fortress.

CHAPTER THREE

THE MIGHTY FORTRESS

The Psalmist claimed the LORD to be his fortress. Psalm 18:2 is one of my favorite verses in the Bible. It reads, "The LORD is my rock, and my fortress, and my deliverer, my God, my strength, in whom I will trust, my buckler, and the horn of my salvation, and my high tower." Why would anyone need a fortress? There are many reasons why. To better understand the word fortress, a definition from Merriam-Webster's online dictionary is a help. It defines the word fortress as, "a fortified place: STRONGHOLD; especially: a large and permanent fortification sometimes including a town."[1] "Stronghold" is a synonymous word. Understanding this expression sheds more light on this topic. "Stronghold" is defined by the same online dictionary as, "a fortified place, 2a: a place of security or survival."[2] "Fortification" is a means of providing security. How very vital for us to make our homes secure! Merely talking about providing security is of no help. This chapter provides the method and the "know how." As this study begins to shape up, more information on the other essentials of building the home will surface. Why did emperors and empires build forts? They did not build them for decorative purposes, although a fort does provide architectural beauty. There are more valuable reasons for their existence. These reasons emphasize the need and importance of building a fort around a home. It is essential for every home to incorporate the element of the fortress into its design.

WHY DID THEY BUILD FORTS?

Forts were built for various reasons. The first reason, because they provide strength. Hence, they are strongholds. This aspect of the fort is visible throughout the Old Testament books. Judges 6: 2 reads, "And the hand of Midian prevailed against Israel: and because of the Midianites the children of Israel made them the dens which are in the mountains, and caves, and strong holds." A second purpose (in the same verse) is they provided protection from danger. A third good reason, so nations could defend against enemies. Nahum 2: 1 addresses this reason, "He that dasheth in pieces is come up before thy face: keep the munition, watch the way, make thy loins strong, fortify thy power mightily."

A home is a God-ordained, God-initiated institution. It is God's idea. It is God's design and must be guarded carefully against the many lurking dangers. One excellent way to avert every threat is by fortifying the home. God's formula will ensure it of success. However, guarding against any seeming danger is our responsibility.

God initiated the family in the book of Genesis. Back then, in the Garden of Eden, He formed Adam and Eve. Both of them formed the first home. They were "the home." Soon Satan attacked the home. Ever since his downfall, he tries hard to destroy the home. He stuck a wedge between God, Adam, and Eve. He planted the seed of doubt. He made them feel inadequate. He is against everything God does. God established the home. Satan tries to destroy the home. Satan did not esteem his God given position. He was God's chief archangel. Since his fall, he tries to go against everything God creates. Thus, the Bible calls him 'the destroyer.' Adam and Eve floundered with sins of selfishness and unbelief. They succumbed to the wiles of the Devil. In doing so, Adam and Eve sinned against their eternal God. God's loving care protected them from eating of the tree of life. After their fall, had they eaten of the tree of life, they would have found themselves in an unredeemable disposition. God exercised care towards them, protecting them from that danger. God cares for the home. Since God cares for the home, we too must care for it.

Man's totally depraved condition, meant that he could no longer approach God. God hates sin, for sin had caused man to be at enmity with God. Man is incapable of rectifying this broken relationship. Ever since Adam's fall, all men are born sinful. His depraved state has tainted even his most righteous acts. His hands are blood stained.

He stands condemned. Thus, reconciliation has to be both made and met on God's terms. God in His infinite wisdom, set into motion, His gracious plan of salvation. He sought to save man from the terrible web in which he found himself entangled. God decided that through "a seed" he would be able to provide salvation full and free, to all of mankind. In order to accomplish this he would have to use a family.

We understand God established the home. We have come to recognize Satan's goal is to destroy the home. We realize that Satan tries hard to destroy everything God creates. How does he do this? He uses a wide variety of his artillery. With their aid he tries to snuff out every home. Satan's evil desire was for all creatures to worship him. He wanted to be like God. God was going to use the family to bring about His plan of salvation. Through a family, "the Seed" would be born. That "Seed" is none other than the Lord Jesus Christ. Satan knew this to be true. Hence, he has tried long and hard to destroy the family. If he could somehow succeed in his effort to destroy the home, he could then in turn obliterate the plan of salvation.

By the time Noah was born sin had grown, flourished and was rampant. Genesis chapter six states, "And GOD saw that the wickedness of man was great in the earth, and that every imagination of the thoughts of his heart was only evil continually" (Gen. 6: 5). By this time, the sacredness and sanctity of the home was challenged. The Bible says, "There were giants in the earth in those days; and also after that, when the sons of God came in unto the daughters of men, and they bare children to them, the same became mighty men which were of old, men of renown" (Gen. 6:4). Satan tried to snuff out the home. If he could somehow succeed in destroying it, then, the hope of the promise of salvation through the promised 'seed' would also be shattered. Christ would not be born. This is Satan's simple equation. What dire consequences would have resulted if he had managed to crush the home! His equation: no seed = no redeemer, would prove to be deadly. While God has His formula to build the home, Satan has his formula, to destroy the home. Through all of this, his ultimate goal is to try to eliminate the Redeemer from his terrible equation.

WHY MUST WE FORTIFY THE HOME?

BECAUSE OF SATAN

All through Israel's history, Satan has tried to destroy the home, the seed. During the days of Noah, he tried to destroy all the families of the earth. God protected Noah, preserving his family from annihilation, or else wickedness would have wiped it out. God chose the man Abraham, to follow Him. Again, He had chosen "a family." God gave Abraham precious promises. He promised to make his family a great nation, and that through his seed all the nations of the earth would be blessed. God promised to take his family to the Promised Land. Later on, God chose Isaac, then Jacob. Each of these families played a pivotal role in the birth of a nation, Israel. Since creation,

Satan did not relinquish the demolition project he had on his agenda. He did not resign from his gruesome desire to destroy the home. History records, how that in New Testament times, Herod attempted to kill Jesus at a tender age. Through a dream, God revealed Herod's malicious plot to Joseph. God protected His Son from Satan's vile ploy and averted him from certain death. He has always succeeded in protecting the home. However, Satan has not given up. He never quits trying. Satan's stratagem has not changed a bit. Even today, he is destroying homes rapidly. He has been very successful in doing so. He will demolish more homes, families, and that too with a vengeance. The reason he does so with a vengeance is because he knows the day of his doom is fast approaching. God has equipped us to fight this deadly enemy. The home is a priced treasure. We must protect it with our very lives. We must do all we can, while we can. We must use the right formula, the right design, the right ingredients, the right strongholds, the right foundation, and the right structure in order to protect it from the wiles of the Devil.

BECAUSE OF SIN

Sin threatens to creep into every home. Sin is one of Satan's key artillery. Some sins have crept into modern society posing a real danger, threatening the survival of the home. These sins could well be:

- The sin of immorality
- The sin of homosexuality

- The sin of open marriages
- The sin of unfaithfulness

Listed above are only a few of the many sins that threaten the survival of the home. We will talk more about these sins in later chapters. These sins have been around since the beginning. Hence, they are not new to man. In our modern society these sins have lifted their head. They have only become more acceptable. We will try to expose some of these sins as we progress in our study. Surely these sins pose serious threats to the existence of our homes. However, they need not shake our foundations or rock our faith. They need not bring fear or despair. When discouragement sets in, the battle is lost. As Christians, we must realize we are on the victor's side. We are more than conquerors through Christ. We will prevail. We have much greater artillery than Satan. We have an inexhaustible reserve and resource.

Remember, Satan is a defeated enemy, so is sin. Sin cannot rule over us. The key to our success lies in trusting in God. It is a matter of walking with God. We must walk by His precepts. We must abide in his care.

BECAUSE OF SITUATIONS

Modern communication has changed the way of life. With the advancement of technology, electronics and computers, both distance and cultures are narrowing their horizons. Television has drastically changed man's way of life. People the world over have changed their dress, music, mannerisms, and even behavior. Modern trends have done away with morality. In the present world, homosexuality, lesbianism and transgender lifestyle has become another norm of life. Contemporary communities do not look at these as sin anymore, neither do they condemn them. Modern society demands all of mankind to be indiscriminating against these groups of people. Modern trends and religions do not condemn these sins, they condone it. Vice has become virtue, virtue has become vice.

Tolerance is propagated and practiced more these days. The common man, organizations and governments support these groups. They say it is a way of life. They claim, "Every human being has the right to choose to live the way he likes". Since when did God give man the authority to amend His standards and morals? These relationships are not normal. This explains why none of these relationships existed from the beginning. God made woman for man. All other relationships are unnatural, unbiblical and immoral.

An upsurge of these unusual, unbiblical patterns of life has surfaced. Societies, leaders, and courthouses want men to accommodate these groups of people. They ask that we be favorable to such trends. The Bible does tell us that we are to be kind to all men. This does not mean we can condone sin. Sin must be called sin. The Bible draws a line. It sets boundaries. Believers must adhere to its precepts. Christians are not to be beguiled by the shifting trends, or the waves of time and tides of change. We are not to be sucked into the whirlpool of modern beliefs. For the Christian, the Bible stands as his only authority for all faith and practice. It is what we live by. We must be willing to live by it and die for it.

REASONS FOR FORTIFICATION

Forts were built to protect a city or nation from enemies. Warfare was different in Biblical times. Early warfare did not have the kind of weaponry or ammunition we have available today. Soldiers used swords, slings and other artillery to wage warfare. Some soldiers walked to the battleground while others who rode on horseback, were part of the cavalry. Though there have been some drastic changes in the strategies of warfare with the increasing use of modern weaponry and ammunition, the purposes of warfare are still the same. Here are some reasons why nations wage wars. They do so because of: pride, sin, selfishness, greed, power, and position. These sins now attack and target the home. They are part of Satan's armory since the beginning. He has always used them to attack the home.

The supreme enemy of God is Satan. He is the god of the godless. He is the chief enemy of the home. He works tirelessly trying to destroy the home. He is not tired of fighting this battle. He aims to bring down every home, with no regard to whether a home is a Christian home or not. Since he has such a vehement destructive desire to tear down every home, we ought to do something to protect it from his animosity. What can we possibly do to protect it? Notice carefully the elements that comprise a fort. They will provide us some helpful tips towards fortifying our homes.

WHAT ELEMENTS COMPRISED A FORT?

THE WALL

The wall played an important role in fortification. Walls were big, broad, tall and strong. They were so big that in some cities such as Jericho, houses could be built on them. Rahab's house was built upon the walls of Jericho. She was the woman that dared to hide the Israeli spies, though it meant risking her own life while doing so. Some historians claim that six chariots could run alongside each other on some city walls. Walls protected the city. They were built with brick or timber. Walls were high, thus they provided a vantage point to help detect the threats of an enemy early enough so as to prepare them for any oncoming threat. A tower was another element integrated in the design of the city wall. Some city walls had many towers built at certain points along a city wall.

The positive benefits of walls are quite obvious. They helped provide security for the people inside a city. On the other hand, they posed an obstacle for those who tried to invade the city. Walls sometimes encased rivers or coastlines. One great example of fortification is the Great Wall of China. Wikipedia, the free encyclopedia explains some extraordinary details concerning this Great wall:

The Great Wall stretches over approximately 6,400 km (4,000 miles)[3] from Shanhaiguan in the east to Lop Nur in the west, along an arc that roughly delineates the southern edge of Inner Mongolia, but stretches to over 6,700 km (4,160 miles) in total.[4] At its peak, the Ming Wall was guarded by more than one million men.[5] It has been estimated that somewhere in the range of 2 to 3 million Chinese died as part of the centuries-long project of building the wall.³

China took great efforts to build this defensive wall as it provided a means by which they could protect their nation. Great pains must be taken to defend our homes from the enemy. Huge investments were made to erect these great fortifications. Colossal investments of time, energy and prayer must be devoted to fortify our homes. A fort comprised not only of a wall but had other vital elements. One such element is the gate.

GATES

Gates were the only points of entry into a city. Gates were big and strong. Everyone had to enter the city through the city gates. Minimizing the entry points into the city provided greater protection. One simple reason gates were used was, when people came in through them, they could be scrutinized. Gates were closed at night and opened in the morning. Traders that arrived after the gates were shut had to wait for the city gates to open up the next day. Enemies could not invade a city until they broke open the gate. Sufficient supplies were stored in a fortified city to sustain itself for at least two years. Enemies that tried to invade it had to besiege it. Invaders would oft camp outside the city wall for many months or years. When the city ran out of supplies, they ran out of options so they were forced to open up the gates. Enemies then could enter in and invade it.

TOWERS

Towers were built on city walls or integrated within the design of the wall. They were built tall enough to provide a good sentinel. High towers are referred to numerous times in the Bible. "High tower" as the name suggests, provided an extremely good vantage point so soldiers can scout the area for a good distance. If an enemy was found approaching, the watchman could warn the soldiers. This strategy enabled them to be quick to respond to any dangerous situation. They were able to detect any approaching enemy in time.

Understanding the importance of forts sheds light on why cities or nations invested much time, energy and resources towards building these massive structures. God wants us fortify our homes from every threat. Like the watchman on the towers, we must watch out for hazards that may destroy our homes. The fortress provided safety and security. In the spiritual sense, forts are illustrative of the following (1) God's protection (Psalm 18: 2 and Jer. 16: 19.) (2) God's care (2 Sa. 22: 2, 3.) Allow me to quote a verse from each of these points. While talking of God's protection David says (Palm 18: 2), "The LORD is my rock, and my fortress, and my deliverer; my God, my strength, in whom I will trust; my buckler, and the horn of my salvation, and my high tower." God would certainly not extend His protection if He did not care. His loving care is expressed in II Samuel 22: 2 and 3. Verse two reads, "And he said, The LORD is my rock, and my fortress, and my deliverer". He continues to speak of God's care in verse three, "The God of my rock; in him will I trust: he is my shield, and the horn of my salvation, my high tower, and my refuge, my saviour, thou savest me from violence."

If the believer is to fortify the home, he must first build a wall, a hedge, a stronghold or a mighty fortress and a high tower. These protect. They help defend against any possible dangers. These help alert and avert when dangers threaten the home. They do not allow these enemies to creep up upon them unawares. I would like to dig deeper into the use of forts by asking a few more questions. There are questions we must all ask and answers we must find. We want answers. We need them. But here are the questions we must address first. Why are we dwelling on the fortification of cities? How is fortification related to the home? What does it represent?

WHAT IS THIS FORTRESS?

What is this fortress? What is its analogy? Can the believer really build a mighty fortress, literally? What does the Bible have to say about this topic? Can we secure our homes with such a fortress? Let the Bible speak for itself. It has the answers. I would like to refresh your mind by quoting again II Samuel 22: 2, to drive home a key message. In this passage of Scripture David speaks these words when the Lord delivered him out of the hand of his enemies, in fact out of Saul's clutches, "The LORD is my rock, and my fortress, and my deliverer." Let us quote Psalm (18: 2) for the sake of redundancy. In this passage notice the emphasis David makes by re-living the moment of his trial and re-telling the person he depended upon most of all for strength and deliverance, "The LORD is my rock, and my fortress, and my deliverer; my God, my strength, in whom I will trust; my buckler, and the horn of my salvation, and my high tower. This verse has become one of my all-time favorite verses in the Bible. By way of application, we may claim this verse personally, or for the home, or even for a nation. An anonymous writer in the book of Psalms pens the following words in Psalms 91:2, "I will say of the LORD, He is my refuge and my fortress: my God; in him will I trust."

During a difficult time in the history of the church, a great reformer was born. He grew up as a Roman Catholic. "On October 31, 1517, Martin Luther nailed his ninety-five theses to the door of the Cathedral of Wittenberg, Germany. That date was sometimes called the "4th of July of Protestantism."[4] It symbolized the start of the Protestant Reformation." During this distressful time, Luther found in the Great Jehovah of the Old Testament and Jesus Christ of the New Testament, a mighty fortress. *Tanbible.com* has the following words to say about this wonderful hymn and hymn writer: "And the single most powerful hymn of the Protestant Reformation

Movement was Luther's "A Mighty Fortress Is Our God," based on Psalm 46. This hymn became the battle cry of the people, a great source of strength and inspiration even for those who were martyred for their convictions. Its majestic and thunderous proclamation of our faith is a singing symbol of the reformation."[5]

This hymn was inspired by Psalm 46. Luther captured in its lyric the basis of the Christian faith. He encapsulates in it the passion and loyalty portrayed in Psalm 46, which mirrors the zeal of true believers. The hymn "A Mighty Fortress" helped believers of Luther's time go through those tumultuous times.

Presently, the home is in the midst of turbulent times. The home is caught confronting in a perilous storm. This hymn is reminiscent of the fact that God is still "a mighty fortress." During Luther's time, God was a fortress able to shelter believers and their homes from the attacks of the Roman Catholic Church. God is still "the same, yesterday, today and forever." He can shelter the home from the vicious attacks of the foe it faces. The libretto of this hymn is worth reviewing, so read on carefully,

A Mighty Fortress Is Our God

> A mighty fortress is our God, A bulwark never failing;
> Our helper He amid the flood, Of mortal ills prevailing.
> For still our ancient foe Doth seek to work us woe-
> His craft and power are great, And, armed with cruel hate,
> On earth is not His equal.

Did we in our own strength confide, Our striving would be losing,
Were not the right man on our side, The man of God's own choosing.
Doth ask who that may be? Christ Jesus, it is He-
Lord Sabaoth His name, From age to age the same,
And He must win the battle.

And though this world with devils filled, Should threaten to unto us.
We will not fear, for God hath willed His truth to triumph through us.
The prince of darkness grim, We tremble not for him-
His rage we can endure, For lo, his doom is sure:
One little word shall fell him.

That word above all earthly powers, No thanks to them, abideth;
The Spirit and the gifts are ours Through Him who with us sideth.
Let goods and kindred go, This mortal life also-
They body they may kill; God's truth abideth still:
His kingdom is forever.[6]

I began this chapter asking the question, what is a fortress? At this point, I choose to rephrase it. Permit me to ask the same question with these reshaped words, "Who is our fortress?" Does it sound right? I make no mistake. The words I use here are on purpose. They are the right words that frame my question. "Who is our fortress?" All through this chapter, I have tried to briefly illuminate the idea of building a fortress only with the single intention of trying to aid our understanding of how this compares with the building of the home. We cannot build a fortress or a hedge around our home in reality. What then is the idea of explaining all this? The purpose of all this explanation about the fort is single and unique, simply to point you to a person. That person is that fort. That person or fort for the believer is the Lord Jesus Christ. When God's protective hedge surrounds our home, the home is truly safe.

Christ is that fortress. We need him. Christ alone can help make our homes: stand the test of time and weather the storms of life. If our home are to last a lifetime, WE NEED JESUS! He is the mighty fortress of our homes. An unknown songwriter articulates, "With Christ in my vessel I can smile at the storm." How true a statement that is! The Bible has the story of how the disciples faced a terrible situation when they were caught in the midst of a horrendous storm. Jesus lay asleep. To them, it seemed He didn't care. When they ceased fighting the storm with human strength, hoping to keep the boat afloat, they cried out to Jesus. In their utter despair, they woke up out of child-like deep slumber. He gently rebuked them for their faithlessness. Then turning to the storm, spoke to it in a commanding voice saying, "Peace be still." Thus the song writer wrote, "With Christ in my vessel I can smile at the storm." We have Jesus on our side. We surely cannot lose hope. The home was God's idea. He instituted it. He initiated it. He will help us build it, and build it we will. With Jesus as our fort, our home can stand strong. With Jesus as our fort our home can rest secure.

CHAPTER FOUR

ROCK SOLID FOUNDATION

Are foundations important? Must we have a rock-solid foundation? Does it really matter what we build our homes on? Who or what must be the foundation? What must be the right ingredients? A look at some statistics provides answers to some of the above questions.

STARTLING STATS

Statistics provide a specific yet approximate idea of current thoughts and issues. They make comparisons. Studying statistics can help monitor change. "The recent 2002 CENSUS BUREAU DIVORCE STATISTICS suggest that 50% of all married couples in US will be seeking a DIVORCE ATTORNEY."[1] This is a startling fact. It is a very scary statistic. Why are so many marriages falling apart? Why are lasting marriages a rarity? Why do homes crumble? Why is crime on the rise? Why do children become drug addicts?

Why do they live aimless lives? Why is homosexuality and lesbianism on the rise? Sin of every kind manifests itself in greater measure each day. Could there be a valid reason? Statistics reveal:

> **In Southern California** the divorce rate is believed to be even higher, somewhere in the neighborhood of **60-75%**.
> The number of **US divorces in 2000** was 957,200, compared to 944,317 in 1999, and 947,384 in 1998.
> The number of divorced people in the population more than quadrupled from 4.3 million in 1970 to 18.3 million in 1996.[2]

These are frightening numbers. But, there is more sad news. There are 9.7 million Americans living with an unmarried different-sex partner and 1.2 million American living with a same-sex partner. 11% of unmarried partners are same-sex couples.[3] Why are these facts so worrisome? Why are these numbers so large? It is surprising how trends capture the minds and bodies of young people and adults in a perilous whirlpool of destruction. Satan has lured the world into giving people pleasure but not without a heavy price tag. He offers them seeming, temporary joy in exchange for the certain doom. He makes people exchange: true love for loneliness, dreams for delusion, also hope for hopelessness. He robs man of everything good in exchange for all the bad and the ugly. Everything Satan offers comes with a costly price tag. Some of his price tags include: broken homes, broken hearts, shattered dreams, traumatized families, sexual diseases, HIV, AIDS, wrecked lives, children out of wedlock, single mums, single dads, and insecure children. These are a few of the many ripples caused by a home that crumbles.

As a child I loved to hike, go biking, play by a pond or stream. I engaged in almost everything normal boys did. It was fun to be a boy. I remember how I threw a small, chipped tile, horizontally into a pond. This little tile, skipped on the surface of the water. Boys would compete to see how many times their little tile skipped. I remember dropping a stone into a pond. Once the stone hit the water it caused a small ripple. I watched the effect the little stone had. It caused a ripple. I did not realize how this could relate to life. Now I see the impact one little stone had on the water. The ripple grew in size, until it became so big, I lost track of it. This is the kind of effect sin has on our lives. Satan makes us believe that his offer is genuine. When we accept his offer, the ripple effect begins. Once sin has caused a ripple, it affects so many lives. Another statistic unveils, other repercussions affecting children coming from a crumbling home or broken family. It states:

> Studies in the early 1980s showed that children in repeat divorces earned lower grades and their peers rated them as less pleasant to be around.[8] Teenagers in single-parent families and in blended families (stepfamilies) are three times more likely to need psychological help within a given year.[9]
>
> "Compared to children from homes disrupted by death, children from divorced homes have more psychological problems."[10] Children of divorce are four times more likely to report problems with peers and friends than are children whose parents have kept their marriages intact.[11] People

who come from broken homes are almost twice as likely to attempt suicide than those who do not come from broken homes.[4]

It is tragic to see the outcome of a broken home. How is it, that society is not moved to do something about it? Don't we see, hear, or feel the pain of these children? Notice further:

> Children of divorce are about two to three times more likely to grow up with a parent who struggles with alcoholism than children from an intact marriage.[13] Children of divorced parents are roughly two times more likely to drop out of high school than their peers who benefit from living with parents who did not divorce.[14] Girls from a broken family are twice as likely to become teen mothers than girls living with biological parents who have not divorced.[15]
>
> A child living in a female-headed home is 10 times more likely to be beaten or murdered."[16]
>
> Seventy percent of long-term prison inmates grew up in broken homes.[17]
>
> Of the juvenile criminals who are a threat to the public, three-fourths came from broken homes.[18] Fully 75 percent of those charged with homicide had parents who were either divorced or had never been married at all; that number rises to 82 percent of those charged with nonviolent larceny offenses.[19]
>
> A survey of 108 rapists undertaken by Raymond A. Knight and Robert A. Prentky revealed the 60 percent came from female-headed homes, 70 percent of those describable as 'violent' came from female-headed homes. 80 percent of those motivated by 'displaced anger' came from female-headed (single-parent) homes.[5]

Why The Home Crumbles

These statistics may seem unreal, but they are the glaring facts facing us. We care about people dying from starvation. We ought to care. We concern ourselves with those going through severe malnutrition. We ought to be concerned. We feel for those people struck by a tornado, a hurricane, a storm, a flood, and a Tsunami. We ought to have feelings for those who go through such disasters. Numerous organizations involve in doing a good work, trying in all earnestness to help the orphans, the homeless, and the underprivileged. Who will care for the homes that are crumbling? Who is going to feel for the children that face the tremors of a falling home? Are we asleep, shortsighted, or indifferent to these dire needs? We rush aid to, a New Orleans affected by a flood. Thousands of people responded to the rescue of New Orleans to abet in rebuilding fallen homes. When are we going to wake up to the unheard cries of the millions, to the sounds of homes that crumble? Something must be done immediately. We must wake up before it is too late!

The present statistics are horrifying. Yet, many plunge into relationships without giving much thought to what the future holds for them. One wonders, "Aren't they aware of these prevailing dangers?" Selfish, fleshly desires aim at gratifying the immediate bodily needs. Lust blinds people's vision bringing far-reaching consequences. These consequences endanger the lives of those involved in these sins. They place the lives of their kids in grave perils. No thought is given to the serious repercussions that follow a home built on an insecure foundation. Thus, this chapter seems to fit here, much like a missing piece of a jig-saw puzzle. There is great need for homes to be built upon a "Rock-Solid Foundation." Laying such a foundation can only be accomplished by returning to the Bible. The Bible, God's Holy Word, has the guidelines to help establish homes. Every home needs a sure foundation. It must be built on solid Rock.

What or who is this Rock? The answer is clear. Examining a few Scripture verses leads to one revelation. The "rock" is the Lord Jesus Christ. He is that Rock. He is that sure foundation. Samuel writes in I Samuel 2:2, "There is none holy as the LORD: for there is none beside thee: neither is there any rock like our God." The Church was established upon (Mt. 16:18) "this rock" referring to Jesus Himself. It was and is being built upon Jesus. If any man builds his home on "this Rock", it shall stand firm. We need this foundation for our homes more than ever before. Build your home, on the Rock of Ages. The hymn writer verbalized his firm faith in this truth, "On Christ the solid rock I stand, all other ground is sinking sand, all other ground is sinking sand." So, build your home on the "ROCK."

A STROLL BACK DOWN MEMORY LANE

Bible college days were exciting. These were years; I soaked in a great deal spiritually. For the first eight to ten years of my life, I was without Jesus, though I was from a so-called Christian home. After salvation, a lack of true Bible teaching during the next twelve years of my life, made me spiritually malnourished. Calvary Baptist

Bible College and Seminary (Bangalore, India), prepared for me a huge spiritual banquet that awaited my arrival, each day. I ate of God's Word like a starved child. These were years; my life in Jesus took a new turn. Amazing years, during which I slowly, but surely built a solid foundation.

The Bible stresses the importance of building slowly but surely. Isaiah 28:10 reads, "For precept must be upon precept, precept upon precept; line upon line, line upon line; here a little, and there a little." The context of this verse addresses drunkards that scoffed at Isaiah's warnings. They ask, "Who is Isaiah trying to teach knowledge to?" They add, "Who is he trying to help understand instruction? Does he consider us to be just weaned?" They interrogated Isaiah, because he used redundancy as a method to teach them. They felt belittled. They wondered why Isaiah treated them like little children. He uses 'precept upon precept,' a method they considered was meant, only for children.

Reiteration is a method, which can be effectively used in teaching all age groups of people. Recurrence is used to show emphasis. God uses this method of teaching in the Bible. However, these people in Isaiah 28 thought this method inappropriate for them. Thus, they scoffed at Isaiah's teaching. Every house is built by laying one brick upon another, one brick at a time. Each wall takes shape as the mason lays one brick upon another. The home likewise, must be built upon the precepts of God's Word.

A flash back of my life, takes me on an amazing trip. This journey begins in my mother's womb, wherein I was conceived. When I ponder upon how God formed and fashioned me, I am astounded. Miracle after miracle, transformed the little fetus into a tiny baby. Thereafter, hormones triggered different stages of growth. Teenage years brought about new changes. I discovered new facial hair. My voice began to turn gruff, crack up, finally producing in me the voice that I now possess as an adult. Then, in my early adult years, new hormones triggered new emotions. Feelings I seemed to have never had before, surfaced. I remember distinctly, it was my third year in Bible College. The Lord had sparked off a desire in my heart for a helpmate. God triggered a desire for marriage. Looking back, I see how Lord orchestrated every event, every situation, so wonderfully well. Leah had come to Bible College after completing her nursing. "Isn't that strange," I reminisce now. Why would a nurse come to study in a Bible College? Though I had seen Leah for many years, I did not know her on a personal level.

The same girl I had seen for many years in school, and had not taken the time to notice, suddenly caught my attention. She appeared so beautiful. Why is it, now she attracted my attention? To tell you the truth, I felt attracted to her. I began to develop feelings for Leah. I prayed about this. I asked God if He would give me Leah for a wife. How my mind thought differently during those days, surprises even me. These were the early adult years of my life. I was about to embark on a wonderful journey, a roller coaster ride that would try every emotion and character I possessed. The "distance" I traveled from the time the thought sparked in my mind, to the time I literally asked her to marry me, was both a very long and a scary journey.

Godly teachers expounded the Word of God. Miss Olive Brittian, my Christian Ethics professor, taught me the importance of prayer, from the Scriptures. She somehow instilled into each lesson, the importance of finding the will of God. Finding the will of God is vital, but following through is key to pleasing God. I learned this lesson well. It stuck. Knowing the will of God became all-important. This desire, like an anchor, grounded my new life of faith. I struck gold the first time I came across Proverbs 3: 5-7a, "Trust in the LORD with all thine heart; and lean not unto thine own understanding. In all thy ways acknowledge him, and he shall direct thy paths. Be not wise in thine own eyes." Acknowledging God in every detail of my life became a pattern. I realized, without Jesus, nothing would be a blessing.

The Lord stirred in my heart the desire for a helpmate. I prayed a lot about this. To be honest, laying this desire at the altar, was both difficult and scary. I wanted God to approve my desire. "There's something radically wrong about this kind of prayer," I thought. I had to just trust God with my life. I had to trust His will. I had to believe His will was always the best. I left this prayer at the altar. I let it sit there for a while.

Before these feelings surged, I had no idea as to when I would get married. I did trifle my time thinking of who I might marry. As

I mentioned before, I had no thoughts of finding a wife in the near future. Bible College days stirred within me a passion for learning. Like the apostle Paul, I had one desire, the desire, "That I may know Him." I purposed in my heart that nothing would distract me from getting my Master of Divinity degree. Earning a degree was not my main goal of life. It just kept me studying God's Word. Enrolling as a student at Calvary Baptist Bible College and Seminary, made what I was doing important. It made me have a purpose in life. Most of all I enjoyed the opportunity to learn about my precious Savior. Not even marriage was on my mind, at this time. I asked God to lead me. Isaiah reminds me of God's mind on matters in 55:8, "For my thoughts are not your thoughts, neither are your ways my ways, saith the LORD." How strange, God was about to change my plans.

This verse proved to be true in my life. My desire to pursue my studies was interrupted. After completing my Batchelor of Theology, God had sparked in me a love for Leah. Aunty Olive, my Christian Ethics teacher had taught me a very precious truth. In one lecture she said, "It is never too early to pray for a life partner." She had stressed the importance of praying for this. She emphasized the significance of making the right choice in finding a wife. The pastor's wife plays a very important role if he is to succeed in the ministry. I was training for the ministry. Three years into praying for God's choice of a woman, God had struck a match. He had lit a desire in my heart to get married, to begin a home. It is strange how that, my plans were not God's plans. I had to submit to His plan.

God ignited the desire for a new kind of friendship. I was falling in love with Leah each day. This new desire grew more with each passing day, with each passing moment. I sought God's will for my life. I wished to start this new phase of my life on a sure foundation. I was determined to have this decision anchored on a firm foundation. I began to love Leah dearly, but I had no way of telling if she loved me. I did not approach her for a long time. These were days in which, I prayed earnestly asking God to lead me each step of the way. I wanted God to give me the woman He had made just for me.

I asked God, "What is your desire for my life?" I surrendered my life to Jesus. I surrendered my will to Him. Whatever He chose for me would always be the very best. Trusting His leading, I waited for His perfect time for me to approach Leah. Determined, in my heart to seek God from the very beginning, I prayed, asking God to reveal if Leah was the right girl for me. I decided back then, I was going to build my home on the right foundation. What is this right foundation? In time, we will find that out.

At this point, let me share some important traits God showed me, while I sought to start a relationship, essentials like green signal lights, indicating, I was heading in the right direction. First, both Leah and I were saved. The Bible warns believers of entering into a relationship with the unsaved, (II Corinthians 6:14), "Be ye not unequally yoked together with unbelievers: for what fellowship hath righteousness with unrighteousness? and what communion hath light with darkness?" Second, God had called us both to serve Him. Third, we were of marriageable age. These were the positive pointers.

I can never overemphasize the value of laying a right foundation. Let me show you the danger of not doing so. God respects every home (believers and unbelievers) alike. God's Word declares, "Marriage is honorable in all." The big difference however, is unbelievers do not know God, neither do they have a right foundation. This makes their home very precariously poised. The India Journal had a story in its Friday, 10, 2008 issue that startled me. It reads:

> PORTER RANCH, CA-Karthik Rajaram was found dead on Oct. 6 in his Porter Ranch home alone with his wife, mother-in-law and 3 sons. Rajaram's wife, Subasari, 39, was a bookkeeper at a pharmacy. The oldest son Krishna, 19, a sophomore at UCLA majoring in business economics was an Honor student at UCLA. Ganesha was 12; and Arjuna, 7. Indra Ramasesham, 69, was found dead in a downstairs bedroom. The 45 years-old, turned the gun on himself after killing his entire family.[6]

What a tragic story! Why did such a gruesome event unfold on this terrible day? Let me give you some details. Rajaram had a Master's degree and previously worked for PricewaterhouseCoopers, a major accounting firm, and for Sony Pictures. Jobless at the time, his finances took a nosedive sending him into a deathly downward spiral, setting him on the path of certain doom. This family was living 'The American Dream.' They lived in a 2,800 square-foot rented house. Mr. Rajaram had sold his home in Northridge in 2006 for a huge profit. Notice more details found in the "India Journal" newspaper that tells of his dream life, "Rajaram had sold the house for $750,000 after paying $274,000 for it nine years earlier, the newspaper said. The Times also said he was reported to have made more than $1 million in 2001 after investing in a venture fund called Nano Universe."[7]

Let me caution you here. Success does not guarantee a solid home. Riches do not ensure a strong home. Wisdom does not assure one of a secure home. Nothing of human origin will provide it with strength, stability or durability. Notice, what went wrong in this man's life, causing him to tragically end the lives of his entire family? His was in a financial crisis. It could be that even though he lost his wealth, he could have survived the crisis of losing his family. What was the cause of his financial collapse? It was probably the recession. It could have also been the loss of his position in society, or the shame or the embarrassment of failure. The possibility, he could not face his family back home in India. But why did he choose to end the lives of all his family members and himself? All of these or more reasons contributed to the death and downfall of his family. His home lacked one vital element. It led to the downfall of his home. His home was not built on the right foundation. This was the vital, missing ingredient. Other homes crumble for various other reasons. Some homes crumble because of emotional or physical (health) crisis. Others literal houses crumble, due to calamities such as floods, famines, tornadoes, hurricanes or earthquakes. All of these could shudder our houses and our homes. Only a home built on the Rock can stand strong, unscathed by these terrors of nature.

The Bible illustrates this fact by a telling a simple story. The Bible has the answers man is looking for. In it are hidden rich treasures, able to help every human being live life successfully. Help is available for every problem, every situation. We must search the pages of the Bible, adhere to its counsel, and obey its precepts.

A SIMPLE ILLUSTRATION

What tragedy awaits those who fail to build their home on a solid rock? Untold misery and pain, pave the path of a home not built on a sure foundation. Jesus, the master builder Himself tells a parable. This parable may be used to apply a priceless truth, in relation to building a strong home. Jesus told the story of the wise man and the foolish man. He uses this illustration to convey a truth, obedience. Obedience to God's Word will always bring blessings. The foolish man built his house upon the sand. In contrast, the wise man built his house upon the rock. Both men had completed building their houses. Matthew 7: 27, tells of the outcome of these two houses when situations changed. This passage reads, "And the rain descended, and the floods came, and the winds blew, and beat upon that house." Every home, likewise, will face difficult situations. Every home will be tested. The rains, floods, and winds beat upon the house, testing its resilience in every possible way. Despite these circumstances, the wise man's house stood strong. The foolish man's house fell down. He decided to build his house on the sand, basing it on his own wisdom. His house had a shaky foundation, in fact no foundation at all. The last section of the same verse reads, "and it fell: and great was the fall of it." What happened to the wise man's house? Both houses were confronted with the very same circumstances, but the outcome of one was totally different from the other. The wise man's house (Matthew 7: 25) stood tall. What was the secret to its survival? It survived because it was founded upon a rock.

'Sand' is unstable and unreliable. In contrast, 'rock' is solid, sturdy and dependable. The word 'rock' appears many times in the Bible. Studying a few instances where this word has been used enables us to see the significance of this word. The first reference to the word "rock" is found in Exodus 17:6, "Behold, I will stand before thee there upon the rock in Horeb; and thou shalt smite the rock, and there shall come water out of it, that the people may drink." God dramatically delivered Israel from Egypt. Exodus records the historic exit of God's people Israel from Egypt. Exodus details God's provision and demonstrates God's dependability. God provided food, water and protection miraculously for six hundred thousand men, not numbering the women and children (Exodus 12: 37). God took good care of them for forty years. There were no grocery stores or malls in the burning desert, yet God made sure his children had sufficient to eat and drink. Jesus is oft pictured as the rock that was cleft for us. The "rock" represents God. Life sustaining water flowed out of the rock to quench a thirsty people. God is the one that can give life and sustain life. Only Jesus can satisfy the thirsty soul that longs for a redeemer, a savior. He is the Savior of the world. He is the "rock" that provides a sturdy foundation. Everything that is built upon Him will stand.

A SCRIPTURAL TEACHING

The word "rock" is found numerous times in the Scriptures. Deuteronomy 32: 4 has Moses pen these words, "He is the Rock, his work is perfect: for all his ways are judgment: a God of truth and without iniquity, just and right is he." God is the Rock. This is the conclusion Moses came to. This word is expressive of God's power. It is representative of God's stability. The passage declares God's faithfulness to His covenant. God's was faithful to the promises He made with them and their fathers. Deuteronomy 32:18 alludes to this same fact. This verse is a rebuke to the people of God, "Of the Rock that begat thee thou art unmindful, and hast forgotten God that formed thee." First Samuel chapter two and verse two states, "There is none holy as the LORD: for there is none beside thee: neither is there any rock like our God." David speaks of God as his 'Rock' in Psalms 18:2, "The LORD is my rock, and my fortress, and my deliverer; my God, my strength, in whom I will trust; my buckler, and the horn of my salvation, and my high tower." Asaph affirms that God was his rock as well (Ps 78:35), "And they remembered that God was their rock, and the high God their redeemer."

The subject of the hour in the Gospel of Matthew 16: 18, was the building of the Church. Here, Jesus announces the verity that, He Himself is that rock. God thought it wise to build the church upon a rock, that rock, none other than the Lord Jesus or God Himself. "And I say also unto thee, That thou art Peter, and upon this rock I will build my church; and the gates of hell shall not prevail against it." Matthew uses specific Greek words to distinguish between Peter and Jesus. His choice of words points to Jesus as "the Rock." Paul makes crystal clear that the word 'rock' refers to God (Jesus). He is the "Rock." Read I Corinthians 10:4 to see this truth for yourself, "And did all drink the same spiritual drink: for they drank of that spiritual Rock that followed them: and that Rock was Christ." No further clarification is necessary. Jesus built the Church on the Rock of Ages, that Rock was none other than, Jesus Himself. Both Old Testament and New Testament disclose the fact that the word 'Rock' truly refers to Jesus Christ. Jesus Christ is God. You tell me, how can a house that is built upon God, ever fall? Is it ever possible? The answer to this rhetoric question is capital N, capital O, NO!

A SIMPLE FACT

What then, is the foundation of a true home? Enormous perils threaten the home, every home. How much greater and manifold are the dangers that threaten the home built upon, shifting or sinking sand? Any home built on the wisdom or counsel of man will fall. It may stand tall for a while, even look elegant on the exterior, but it is only a matter of time before it comes crumbling down to the ground. When the storms of life beat upon it, it will fall like a pack of cards. It will fail the test. The consequences of a crumbling home are vast and vicious.

The Bible clearly states that the foolish man built his house upon the sand. We too, will be numbered with the foolish, if we choose to build our home on the insecure wisdom, whims and fancies of this world. We cannot build our homes on uncertainties. The stakes are too high, the risks too burdensome. Hoping to make it somehow isn't good enough. Trying hard to keep the home from collapse is a fleeting endeavor. Mustering up courage to make it work is worthless. Seeking the counsel of the world would be calamitous. Following the trends of this world is too treacherous. It is too grave a matter to gamble with. Building a home is a serious task.

Many seek to build a house. There is one major difference between a house and a home. A house is built with bricks but a home is built with lives. Destroyed houses can be rebuilt but a broken home is too hard to salvage. Hence, no risks should be taken. We have one life to live, one opportunity to build our homes, and build it right, we must. The Bible has the answers. It is the written word of God. Jesus is the Living Word of God. They are both one and the same, inseparable. Its words are life because they originate from

God Himself. Are we willing to use it as our compass to charter our course? Are we willing to use it as our guide, the builder's manual? By simply abiding by its precepts, we can lay a firm foundation, a right foundation. Jesus is that foundation. No home or life built upon Him will ever fail. So build your home on "the Rock," the Lord Jesus Christ!!!!

CHAPTER FIVE

RAISING STRONG PILLARS; REMAINING IN GOD'S PRINCIPLES

Sometimes, a walk around the block is sufficient to view a building in construction. In centuries past, buildings took many months or years to complete. Today, modern machinery has made it possible to raise a building in a much faster time-frame, while still finding ways to make them strong. Raising a home isn't easy. Erecting a building is not a simple chore either. Much planning and preparation is essential to ensure progress. Design aids to, maximize utility of space available. It also adds to the esthetics of the building. All of these play a part. The foundation must be strong. It must be strong enough to hold the building up for a long, long time. Everyone wants to build a durable building with a firm foundation. We want it to last a few decades, hoping it stands strong to serve many generations to come.

A plan, design, or strong foundation is not enough to call any structure a building. A structure must provide shape. Pillars are essential to support the building. Pillars play a vital role in providing strength, beauty and support. They support the roof and walls. Similarly, a home must have pillars. What are some pillars that sustain our home? At this point, I would like to present some pillars that help establish the home.

GOD: THE MAIN PILLAR AND CORNER STONE

The Bible begins by stating the following fact, only God existed before creation (Genesis 1: 1). Notice Genesis 1: 1, "In the beginning God…" God always existed. God initiated creation. He chose to make Adam and Eve. He desired to have fellowship with man. The idea of creation was all His idea. He created man and this beautiful world we now enjoy.

Everything began with God. All creation rests upon Him. God's creative genius is clearly visible in: all of creation, creatures, man, the home, Israel, the tabernacle, the temple and the Church. He instituted all of these. He sustains all things by His power. He holds them up. In the study below, we will examine a few important things God formed. God Himself is our first pillar. Paul, writes of His sustaining power in Colossians 1: 16-17, which says, "For by him were all things created, that are in heaven, and that are in earth, visible and invisible, whether they be thrones, or dominions, or principalities, or powers: all things were created by him, and for him: And he is before all things, and by him all things consist." Without God, everything would fall apart. The Bible declares that God holds the world together. If He can keep the world together, He surely CAN keep the home.

GOD FORMED MAN

God created man with His own hands. The Psalmist describes God's creative acts as His "Handy works." Man is not a by-product of evolution. He is the direct result of God's creation. He did not evolve from a monkey over billions of years. The Bible describes man's origin wonderfully well. Genesis 2: 7 says, "And the LORD God formed man of the dust of the ground, and breathed into his nostrils the breath of life; and man became a living soul." It takes more faith to believe the evolution concoction than it takes to believe God's lucid account of creation. This is the only truthful and logical story, told by God Himself. It is easier for me to believe the Creator's story of creation than for me to believe the creature's tale of it. Either, God or man is lying in telling the creation story. I know God cannot lie. This conclusion makes it quite obvious that man's tale of creation is a plain lie. God made man for a purpose. He formed man, so He could fellowship with him. He desired a special, unique relationship. This relationship was unlike any other. Revelation 4: 11, states God's goal for this relationship. It reads, "Thou art worthy, O Lord, to receive glory and honour and power:

for thou hast created all things, and for thy pleasure they are and were created." God has a supreme desire for his creation of man. It is not aimless evolving of creature. Though God wanted to have pleasure in His relationship with man, He did not force this relationship. He found man unhappy. This situation troubled God. He sought to resolve man's emptiness.

GOD FORMED WOMAN

God saw that Adam was unhappy. God did not make man to live an aimless life. He wants man to involve in two things: a walk and a work. Adam's walk with God was special. While his walk displayed his intimacy with God, His work proved his love for God. Adam named all the animals God had created. This was part of his God-given job. While he obediently performed this chore, he soon discovered that in all of God's creation, he did not find a companion for himself. He did not find a friend, a help meet for himself. God saw his plight and decided, "It is not good that the man should be alone; I will make him a help meet for him" (Gen. 2: 20b). God graciously filled Adam's void, by forming for him, a help meet and companion. He did so by causing Adam to fall into a deep sleep. Then, He took one of his ribs, to form Eve. God walked Eve down the aisle of that first great wedding. He gave away the first bride. He presided over the first marriage ceremony. Genesis 2: 22 reads, "And the rib, which the LORD God had taken from man, made he a woman, and brought her unto the man. To this beautiful gift, Adam responded saying (v.

23), "And Adam said, This (is) now bone of my bones, and flesh of my flesh: she shall be called Woman, because she was taken out of Man." God gave him a companion, a true friend and help meet. The woman God gave him both complemented and completed him. This couple was pronounced, "Man and wife." They formed the first home. Marriage was the first institution God ordained. It ought to be our first priority after God.

GOD FORMED THE HOME

When God saw the need of Adam's heart, He fashioned Eve. By doing so, He met the need of his heart. He brought this couple together. Thus, He instituted the home. I believe it is important to understand the priority of the home. The home primarily consists of a husband and wife. God enlisted some rules in order to make man's home a blessing. Abiding by God's laws always brings blessings. Blessings however, should never be measured or valued in proportion with material things. Blessings are not to be deciphered in terms of material possessions. God's blessings are vast and varied. Sometimes, God's blessings are merely spiritual. Remember, every good gift and every perfect gift comes from God. God's bestows upon us the blessings of joy, peace, happiness and love. These blessings can never be bought with money. Hence, they are priceless.

Man must realize, God did both initiate and institute, the home. Back in the year 1993, I fell in love with Leah. It was the third of November that year; I finally mustered up enough courage to make my first move towards pursuing a relationship with Leah. I was going to make a bold attempt and ask Leah if she would choose to be my help meet. This was all lurking in my mind and I had not yet proposed to her.

I set off on an errand to find a card at a novelty store. I looked desperately to find a card to communicate my intentions for Leah. I finally found one little card and bought it. I thought was incredible. It was not the most expensive card on the rack, neither was it the biggest one. But it was unique and would serve my purpose well. On its front cover was a picture of a well-dressed cat that stood outside a door of a house. He had an umbrella under his arm. He also held a suitcase in the same hand. Printed on the outside of the card were the words, "Is the door to your heart open." The inside of the card, had only a single line of words, "Can I come in?" I said to myself, "Picture perfect." Both the picture and message were perfectly suited for the occasion. After paying for the card, I strolled back home, musing what I would want to inscribe in its empty space.

Various thought darted through my mind. What words can a man falling in love, pen? "I know, I know," I thought. Coming to a conclusion, I determined I must inscribe on it the words every romantic crusader thinks to say, write or sing, "I Love You." So, I set out on a mission to meticulously carve out the words, "I Love You," on this little card, one hundred and twenty-nine of them in all. Painstakingly, I filled every bit of space inside the card. With a few red roses, the card in my hand, I marched off to Calvary Baptist

Bible College and Seminary prayerfully, hoping to find an opportunity to give these gifts to Leah.

This inexpensive card was now priceless, a work of heart. It was a day I will never forget. Unsure of how Leah would respond to my proposal made me nervous. All day I looked for an opportunity to complete my mission of delivering the card. Time seemed to slip away quickly that day. However, I was confident about one thing, God was onboard this mission. He was working on my behalf. Leah's dad (the principal of the Bible College) usually taught classes from 7: 30 am to 1: 00 pm. On this day, he was out attending to something urgent. Unable to return in time to pick up his children from Bible College, he sent them a message, asking the girls to walk home by themselves. My friend Adrian (classmate) was going to accompany Emma and Leah home. Emma (Leah's sister) was my classmate too. She asked me if I could go with them. Though Leah's house was slightly out of the way, distance did not matter especially on this day. The invitation to escort them home was a welcome proposal I could not pass up for the world. Here was my long awaited, opportunity.

Our Bible College was situated in a small village, on the suburbs of the big Bangalore city. The country setting made us walk to Leah's home through some meandering pathways. It took us a good twenty minutes or more to get to their home. Halfway down the path, I pulled out the card, muttered a prayer, and extended it towards Leah. She took it but said nothing. Mission accomplished. At least she accepted my card.

How I wished, the walk would not end that day. I was glad I had accomplished the first step with God's help. My initial proposal to Leah had been bathed in much prayer. I left the rest in God's hand. Fifty-two days had gone by. There was no answer to my card. Did she accept my proposal or reject it. Her silence made me feel awful. I felt anxious. I needed an answer.

It was the Christmas Eve of 1994. Close to midnight; I finally received my first gift from her. I did not know what was in it. I wonder if this was just a nice way to wrap her answer to say, "Sorry, I am not interested." The suspense seemed too much to bear. I recollect it was the wee hours of the morning on Christmas day. Driving back home, from that Christmas Eve service of Grace Baptist Church felt like an endless journey. I just could not wait to get home that morning. I just couldn't wait to open up my well-packed Christmas gift.

It was a forty-minute drive back home from Church. My feet pressed extra hard on the accelerator pedal. I was nervous. However, I wasn't afraid because I had prayed about this proposal for a while. I felt the peace of God in my heart. Excitement was in the air. People were walking back home from services. They yelled out, "Merry Christmas." Some like me were returning from a mid-night service. Others were drunk. It was their worldly way of celebrating Christmas. They too, shouted out Merry Christmas!

I love Christmas. It is the best time of the year. No matter how hard I tried to get home that night, the drive seemed to take forever. All the way home, my mind paced like an anxious deer. Mixed emotions, thoughts, even a quick dart of doubt shot across my mind. I thought, "What if Leah had refused to accept me as her life partner?" I speculated if she politely had penned the words, "Richard, I am sorry, I am not sure that God wants me to marry you." Or did she write to express her uncertainty by saying, "I need some more time?" Well, I tried to be a man. I even thought, "There are many fish in the ocean." If she refuses me, I will quite definitely find someone else. But, I said to myself, "But, but, I love her. I want her to be my wife." I came to the conclusion, "It is Leah or nobody." This was rather an improper conclusion to come to. It would eliminate God in the equation of my life. I had to submit to His will for my life. He had a help meet just for me. For the moment, the suspense was too much to bear.

MOMENTS OF SUSPENSE

I was in love, I was. I asked myself, "Is she in love with me?" This was a million dollar question. This forty-minute drive home seemed to take for ever. Have you ever watched the clock when you are in a hurry to get some place in a hurry? The hands don't seem to move. Yet, at other times, they seem to fly by. These were those slow moments of my life. I questioned myself, "Has the clock forgotten to tick or has it just frozen?" After finally dropping off each Church member at their respective homes that night, I returned home. I can't recall how I parked my car that day. I don't remember turning off the engine. All I reminiscence, is how I ran the ten feet or so to the door of my house like an Olympic sprinter. Upon getting to my bedroom in world record time, I opened up Leah's gift. At first, my heart sunk finding only a devotional book for a gift. It was "The Streams in the Desert." There was no Christmas card in it. I thought to myself, "Is this all she gave me?" "Can't I just be unthankful for the Christmas gift, on Christmas day," I muttered. Glumly, I flipped the cover page. To my astonishment, there were some writings on the front cover page. Hesitantly, I read each word. It had in it, the answer to my long awaited question. It was 52 days to be exact since I had given Leah the card. I'll share this 'personal note' with you. Here's the long awaited answer Leah had written with her own beautiful fingers, "To, The ONLY ONE I LOVE (Richard). You are the first one I have loved and I will always love you. Your love means a world to me; you are very dear to me. You are in everything I do and say. "I LOVE YOU." I thank God for such a great man, He has given me. I remain yours forever. Leah F (Isa.33: 2; 30:18-21)."

THE BEST CHRISTMAS GIFT EVER

Apart from the Lord Jesus Christ, this was the best Christmas gift I had every received. What joy filled my soul that day! I did not know how to respond, whether to run around the block, shout for joy, or cry. Boy! I was so thrilled. All I could do for the moment was thank God. I thanked my Jesus. I had found my helpmeet. I had found my one true love.

Now, looking back, I wonder, "What did Leah like in me?" I had nothing extraordinary to offer her. I was not the handsomest man on planet earth. Neither was I the strongest or wisest. I wonder what attracted her. All I knew at the time is I was truly undeserving of this beautiful Christmas gift God had given me. He had this gift ready just for me. I only felt utterly unworthy to receive such a splendid gift. Why would God want to give me, a sinner saved by Grace, such a precious gift? "He loves me," I thought. That explains it.

I was still a student at Calvary Baptist Bible College and Seminary, Bangalore, Karnataka, India, with no job. These were special days; days my heart found true love. I was so blessed, blessed to have God and now Leah. I couldn't have asked for more.

Soon thereafter, our families met to fix the date for our engagement. March 7, 1994, was the day fixed for our engagement. Three months later on May 7, 1994, we were married. God had begun a brand new home. From the start, Leah and I sought to include God in our plans. We decided He would always to be the epicenter of our home. Both of us realized the home was His idea. We wanted His blessing on our marriage. How wise to partner with God, the author of marriage and the home. This is not just a novel idea but the right thing to do.

Genesis 2: 24 records some of the rules and regulations God provided to ensure happiness in any marriage, "Therefore shall a man leave his father and his mother and shall cleave unto his wife and they shall be one flesh. And they were both naked, the man and his wife, and were not ashamed." These verses highlight five valuable rules or guidelines. Guidelines are useful. They help guide or steer each of God's children in the right direction. They help keep us on course.

GOD'S RULE ONE: A MAN MUST LEAVE

To ensure happiness in a home or marital relationship, a man must leave his father and his mother. God does not say we are to break up the old relationship between parents and children. He wants to begin a new relationship. He is establishing the new, while retaining the old. Leaving one and cleaving to the other helps safeguard both relationships. When couples do not obey this rule, there is bound to be disharmony. One of these two relationships will suffer, simply by virtue of disobedience to his command. Obeying an all-knowing God is not a foolish thing to do. It is the wisest resolution. The word 'leave' comes from the Hebrew word "`azab (aw-zab'); a primitive root; to loosen, i.e. relinquish, permit, etc." meaning to commit self, fail, forsake, fortify, help, leave (destitute, off), refuse, surely. The suggested interpretation is that man is to loosen his relationship with his parents thereby tightening his relationship with his wife. God intends man to draw close to his wife. Early on in my marriage, I found it hard to leave my parents. Responsibilities as the oldest son, made it hard for me to make this separation happen. I felt a great responsibility to take care of them. However, persuaded by God's Word, I knew leaving them to cleave to my wife was the right decision. So, I left my parent's home in a quest to begin my own. This is the right thing to do. It is the Bible way, God's Biblical pattern. I obeyed God's Word and found much joy in doing so. Leaving home is God's design and desire. Therefore, a man must leave his father and mother and cleave to his wife. Obeying God always brings joy, though the steps of obedience themselves may seem extremely difficult to keep.

GOD'S RULE NUMBER TWO: A MAN MUST CLEAVE

God's word declares the second rule in verse twenty-four; a man must cleave to his wife. For any home to guarantee itself happiness, obedience to God's rule number two is essential. When God instructs us, we must obey without argument, debate, or rationalization. God's Word is indisputable. It has the final say on any subject. God omniscience commands respect and demands obedience. First, a man must leave his father and mother. Secondly, he must cleave to his wife. Herein a new relationship is now established. The woman God gave him becomes part of his life. She fills his every void and satisfies his every longing. He must cleave to her.

The idea of cleave is opposite of the word 'leave.' A home should never be built with the idea (of a husband or wife) of leaving each other at any point in the relationship. God wants this relationship to last a lifetime. Nothing should separate it. Death alone is the single legitimate separator of this relationship. Concerning the word 'cleave' *the Vine's Expository Dictionary of Biblical Words* says this

> Dabaq 1692, "to cling, cleave, keep close." Used in modern Hebrew in the sense of "to stick to, adhere to," dabaq yields the noun form for "glue" and also the more abstract ideas of "loyalty, devotion." Occurring just over 60 times in the Hebrew Old Testament, this term: is found very early in the text, in Gen. 2:24: "Therefore shall a man leave his father and his mother, and shall cleave unto his wife: and they shall be one flesh." This usage reflects the basic meaning of one object's (person's) being joined to another. In this sense, Eleazar's hand "cleaved" to the sword as he struck down the Philistines 2 Sam. 23:10. Jeremiah's linen waistcloth "clung" to his loins, symbolic of Israel's "clinging" to God Jer. 13:11. In time of war and siege, the resulting thirst and famine caused the tongue "to cleave" to the roof of the mouth of those who had been so afflicted.[1]

Thus, the word 'cleave' carries the idea of permanence. God established the marital relationship to be between one man and one woman. It is to be enjoyed and must be a life-long relationship. Of course, in our present world people want to have a cheap fling. This is slang, for a no-tie kind of a relationship. They want to enjoy the relationship but not have it rigidly anchored in a commitment. People want to enjoy the intimacy of pleasure marriage brings without any pain or price. They want the pleasure but are unwilling to make the promise or pledge.

Such an evil desire distorts their every perception of this God-initiated relationship. Their distorted thinking has made them arrive at these conclusions: marriage is a burden; children are an expense. They want the pleasure of marriage without having to first make the pledge. God has set boundaries to protect the enjoyment of bodily pleasures. People want the pleasure but are not willing to seal the deal. They do not want to be tied down with one person, that too, for the rest of their lives. They have come to believe, making this commitment means to loose their freedom. In choosing to believe this lie, they become slaves to the sin of selfishness. They become slaves of the devil. This is not God's plan or design for a lasting home. This is not God's goal for marriage. God wants one man and one woman to enjoy deep intimacy. He wants us to enjoy the pleasures marriage has to offer. One of God's great attributes is His faithfulness. God wants us to be like him, "faithful." Another great attribute He possesses is His immutability. Immutability is the quality of not changing. He always remains the same. He never changes. He wants us to emulate His faithfulness and loyal commitment to our life partners. God faithfulness and immutability makes us not be afraid of our relationship with Him. Our faithfulness and loyalty in our marriage provides security to the other partner. This security is vital if we want our marriage to succeed.

GOD'S RULE THREE: A MAN MUST BECOME ONE

God instructs man about the next ideal in this special relationship. God wants man to become one with his wife. Charles R. Swindoll in his book, *Strike the Original Match*, writes elegantly about this aspect, "Becoming one flesh suggests a process, not an instant fact. Two people with different backgrounds, temperaments, habits, scars, feelings, parents, educational pursuits, gifts, and interests don't immediately leave a wedding ceremony in perfect unity. The process begins there, however. And it is a lifelong project requiring wisdom, understanding, and knowledge."[3]

Charles R. Swindoll calls this aspect of the marital relationship "unity." Leah and I had so many differences. Yet, to live in harmony meant, despite our differences we are to bring ourselves to synchronize everything in our lives. God wants husbands and wives to be one. Leah was born in Bombay, India. I was born in Bangalore, Karnataka, India. Leah grew up in a Baptist family, and I in a nominal Christian home. We both ate different kinds of food. The only thing in common was we both had graduated from the same school. Our purpose and philosophy of life was so different. God brought two uniquely different people together in marriage. It always amazes me when I think about it. This is nothing short of a miracle. In time, Leah and I have learned to understand each other. We have made adjustments. We have both tried to work towards common goals. We have tried to acclimatize our differences. God has brought us together in many ways. Fourteen years down the road we still are learning to become one.

Many couples are not willing to make compromises. They are unwilling to give in, or make some sacrifices. When couples fail to become one in every sense of the word, the marriage suffers.

Oneness brings two people to walk in unity. God alone can help us become one.

GOD'S RULE FOUR: A MAN MUST BE INTIMATE

Intimacy is a pleasure only permitted within the perimeters of marriage. Notice what the Bible says about intimacy (Gen 2:25), "And they were both naked, the man and his wife, and were not ashamed." Sin brings shame. Sin when committed brings the feeling and fear of guilt. But, marriage is not an unholy relationship. Hebrews 13:4 attests to this fact, "Marriage is honorable in all, and the bed undefiled: but whoremongers and adulterers God will judge." God sanctions sex within marriage, while He judges (sin) sexual immorality outside of marriage.

Sexual pleasure outside of marital boundaries brings manifold burdens one must bear. It has brought much pain, sickness, disease and even death. God always give us persistent, permanent pleasure while the devil gives us problems to accompany the pleasures he gives. The Devil robs one of bliss only to burden. He plucks away our happiness to plunge us into despair. Man, is so gullible. He is quick to become an easy prey to all of Satan's ploys.

Don't misconstrue God's wonderful gift of marriage. Enjoy it to the fullest. He wants a husband to find intimate pleasure in his wife. He wants the wife to enjoy great bodily pleasure with her own husband. God did not place boundaries to rob you of pleasure but to protect you, so you can enjoy it fully and for a long time. Take time to be intimate. Treasure these intimate moments. Since marriage is a bond in the flesh, these fleshly desires are God given. He gave them for our pleasure. Paul gives us a tip about intimacy. In order for a man and woman to enjoy ultimate pleasure, they must consider their body not their own but as belonging to the other partner. This is an act of unselfishness. To enjoy complete intimacy, each partner must desire to satisfy the other. To love is to give, not so much to receive. Love is an emotion that must find an expression. It must become an action. Such love brings joy and satisfaction.

Finally, Paul reminds us that our body is not our own (I Corinthians 6:19), " What? know ye not that your body is the temple of the Holy Ghost which is in you, which ye have of God, and ye are not your own?" Not only does our body belong to each other. It primarily belongs to God. We do not have the right to do what we like with it. He thus warns us to (I Corinthians 6:18), "Flee fornication. Every sin that a man doeth is without the body; but he that committeth fornication sinneth against his own body." Our body is the "Temple of the Holy Ghost." Paul continues to write in verse twenty giving a more supreme reason for this calling: "For ye are bought with a price, therefore glorify God in your body, and in your spirit, which are God's." Christ purchased us by paying a price for us. He paid with His own blood. It is needful for us to keep our bodies holy and pure for God and our spouses. God desires us to be intimate with our partners. We must glorify Him in this area as well.

GOD IS A DEPENDABLE PILLAR

God is the foundation of everything. He is the pillar of the home, a figurative fact found to be true during Israel's exodus from Egypt. Pharaoh finally let Israel go. When Israel reached the Red Sea, they faced an impregnable obstacle, or so it seemed. Surrounded by mountains, pursued by the Egyptian army, the Red Sea glaring them in the eye left them with no options. Exodus 14: 11 records their faithless cry, "And they said unto Moses, Because there were no graves in Egypt, hast thou taken us away to die in the wilderness? wherefore hast thou dealt thus with us, to carry us forth out of Egypt?" They continued their murmurings and complaints, "Is not this the word that we did tell thee in Egypt, saying, Let us alone, that we may serve the Egyptians? For it had been better for us to serve the Egyptians, than that we should die in the wilderness." When the human eye sees obstacles, God sees an opportunity. When they saw the mountain, God saw a miracle in the making. When they saw the Sea before them, God saw it opportune to give them a song soon after. When they saw the enemy behind them, God saw an entrance before them, in the sea. God always has a strategy, a way of escape. He has the perfect plan in place. They saw the adversary, God saw the adventure.

He was about to take them on the greatest adventure of their life. It would be like an epic adventure through the world's greatest aquarium. They would walk right through the raging sea which stood as a glass on either side of them. He will work wonders. Faith alone can see through the hurdles, the obstacles, and the impossibilities. Faith sees God, while fear sees failure. Faith finds hope, while fear finds hopelessness and helplessness. Faith sees but unbelief blinds. Faith trusts but unbelief doubts.

Before God performed the great miracle of parting "The Red Sea," He did something so remarkable. Exodus 14:19-20 captures this remarkable fete in the following words, "And the angel of God, which went before the camp of Israel, removed and went behind them; and the pillar of the cloud went from before their face, and stood behind them: And it came between the camp of the Egyptians and the camp of Israel; and it was a cloud and darkness to them, but it gave light by night to these: so that the one came not near the other all the night." God, their pillar, protected them. If God could sustain his people (Israel) from certain disaster and doom, He is well able to protect the home. He is able to sustain a relationship, lead us to victories in our marriage. Every home needs Him. Every home needs Him to be that dependable, immovable pillar. If God is our pillar, our home is sure to be anchored to last.

GOD'S WORD: ANOTHER GREAT PILLAR

Another great pillar that helps sustain the home is God's Word. God and God's Word are inseparable. Jesus is the Living Word; the Bible is the Written Word. If God and His Word are one and the same, His Word is another strong pillar. It is a firm foundation that can be relied upon. It is immovable, unchanging and sure. With this in mind, a human author encapsulates this pillar of strength within human words in the great hymn *The Bible Stands*. The lyrics speak of its indestructible strength and resilience.

THE BIBLE STANDS

The Bible stands like a rock undaunted
'Mid the raging storms of time;
Its pages burn with the truth eternal,
And they glow with a light sublime.

The Bible stands though the hills may tumble,
It will firmly stand when the earth shall crumble;
I will plant my feet on its firm foundation,
For the Bible stands.

The Bible stands like a mountain towering
Far above the works of men;
Its truth by none ever was refuted,
And destroy it they never can.

The Bible stands though the hills may tumble,
It will firmly stand when the earth shall crumble;
I will plant my feet on its firm foundation,
For the Bible stands.

The Bible stands and it will forever,
When the world has passed away;
By inspiration it has been given,
All its precepts I will obey.

> The Bible stands though the hills may tumble,
> It will firmly stand when the earth shall crumble;
> I will plant my feet on its firm foundation,
> For the Bible stands.
>
> The Bible stands every test we give it,
> For its Author is divine;
> By grace alone I expect to live it,
> And to prove and to make it mine.
>
> The Bible stands though the hills may tumble,
> It will firmly stand when the earth shall crumble;
> I will plant my feet on its firm foundation,
> For the Bible stands.[4]

If God is the foundation of everything, His Word also is the foundation of everything. If God is the pillar of our home, His Word equally must be a pillar of our home. When we walk in the light of God's Word, we cannot fail to establish a solid home. The psalmist inscribes these words (Psalm 119: 105), "Thy word is a lamp unto my feet, and a light unto my path." God's Word lights up our way. Its light is sufficient for the next step. God guides His children one step at a time.

God's Word helps us to be surefooted in our walk. It guides our footsteps. Psalm 119: 89 declares a solid truth about God's Word, "For Ever, O LORD, thy word is settled in heaven." God's Word is neither shaky, nor uncertain. It is final in all it says. No one needs delve, doubt, or debate it. It will sustain the home. It is our second strong Pillar for the home.

THE CHURCH: OUR THIRD PILLAR

The Church is another institution initiated by God. It is His idea. Jesus said (Matthew 16:18), "I will build my church." The Church is His bride. He loves it enough to give Himself for it. It is a pillar that effectively sustains the home. God desires His people to meet at church for the following valuable reasons: to worship, to fellowship, to be edified, and to grow. The Church was God's idea. He established it on the Rock, Jesus Christ our Lord. In other words He established it on God Himself. It is an immovable pillar. The Bible confirms this fact in I Tim 3:15, "But if I tarry long, that thou mayest know how thou oughtest to behave thyself in the house of God, which is the church of the living God, the pillar and ground of the truth."

The Church is a pillar that every home must lean upon. Within the walls of the Church, God's Word is expounded. His Word is taught in the church, in every meeting. It is there the believer receives admonition, correction, exhortation, rebuke, and strength. When temptations lure you in, or when tempests sway you around, your faith can be re-established or anchored in God's Word. This anchoring takes place when God's Word speaks to the believer in His Church. Every family must be part of a Bible believing, fundamental, true church of God. It is here the family can grow strong. It is in its premises all the necessary alignments can be made, so we can line up to the Word of God. It is here the family can receive counsel. Hebrews 10:25

exhorts believers to, "Not forsaking the assembling of ourselves together, as the manner of some is; but exhorting one another: and so much the more, as ye see the day approaching." Many dangers threaten the believer. The Church will help the believer stay in touch with God and in track with God's Word.

The Bible warns of the coming of the Lord. The day of the Lord is drawing nigh. Sin is still on the rise. The Devil is working overtime. Believers ought to be on guard. The home is on the verge of extinction. We must anchor it in God, God's Word and God's Church. These pillars will help hold it up, sustain it, and ensure it is rooted strongly in the firm foundation, God Himself. He is the author of life, the home, the family and He is the finisher of our faith. In the Trinity, God the Father, God the Son and God the Holy Spirit form the Divine triangle. Here again, we see God provides us another triangle to help the home stand strong. This triangle that sustains the home consists of these three pillars: God, God's Word and God's Church. This divine triangle can sustain our home. He alone can make our home stand firm. It can be done! Yes, God can make our home "stand firm". Erect these pillars, then your home will STAND FIRM.

CHAPTER SIX

WEATHERING STORMS

Dark clouds began to gather. Strong winds surged, sounding like the terrifying howl of a pack of wolves. What began as a sunny day now looked very gloomy? Branches swayed dancing to the beat of the fierce winds. The palm tree branches beat against each other, sounding like vehement clapping of their hands. Every crack in the door and window, gave out a shirking whistle. Lightning spanned the sky. Deafening thunder roared. Drops of water fell out of the sky. Rain! No man had seen rain ever before. Something unusual, they thought. Probably, this might just be a passing cloud. Oh! No! Not so!

Noah had preached about this rain for a hundred and twenty years. It never did seem to come. Nobody believed his message. They thought, "He is loony. He's off his mind." They ridiculed him saying, "Who are you trying to lie to?" People partied; never anticipating Noah's prediction would ever come true. The Bible says (Matthew 24: 38-39), "For as in the days that were before the flood

Why The Home Crumbles

they were eating and drinking, marrying and giving in marriage, until the day that Noe entered into the ark, And knew not until the flood came, and took them all away; so shall also the coming of the Son of man be. "Join the party, pal?" they cried.

Noah preached righteousness for many decades, but no one heeded his cry. God's grace extended a long, long time. God's day of grace came to an end. God Himself shut the door of the ark. Then, God opened up the heavens. When my son Marcus was a little boy and he saw rain for the very first time in his life, he said, "Daddy, I think Jesus is taking a shower." These were innocent, imaginative words of a three year old child's mind. However, this was no child's play.

Rain began to fall. At first, the kids had a ball. Others joined in. It seemed like a fun thing, why even exciting. Laughter filled the air. Soon, the tone in their laughter changed, mixed with merriment at first, and then mingled with fear. When the rain began to pour much more heavily, children ran home. Women scampered to gather their infants. Men tried to act brave, calming their families. Lightening bolts flashed across the sky. The drops of rain got bigger and heavier.

For forty long days and nights, rain beat upon the earth in a relentless manner, as though God had unleashed His whip upon His rebellious creatures. Storms are not new to us. It is hard to picture God as a wrathful being. One must never forget the balance. God is both loving and holy. His love extends grace (so man can be saved); and yet, His holiness demands justice and judgment.

Water levels rose dangerously high, first a few inches, then a few feet. Fear crept up everyone's spine. Lightning flashed across the sky. Thunder roared like an angry Lion, creating an ever increasing fear. Howling winds cried out with their deafening screeches. People were taken aback. The rain was no longer a fun thing. It looked like the ocean was emptying from the sky. It poured and poured unremittingly, so relentlessly for forty days and forty nights. Only eight survived God's judgment. Noah's family made it through this great and terribly dark, watery days and nights. They survived this universal flood.

Storms come in all kinds of packages. Storms are scary. Storms of life are not scary, if we have God with us while we go through them. Dangers may lurk in our dark and oft lonesome journeys but if God is with us, we have no need to fear. We can go through them. Rebellion stirs up God's wrath. It is a terrible sin which caused God to destroy this world with a flood. Noah's flood is a strong reminder of this fact. We need God through the storms of life. We don't want to fight Him. Our chances of winning are bleak, when we fight God. I want to be on the Lord's side. How about you?

Storms come in many sizes. Wikipedia defines it as, "A **storm** is any disturbed state of an astronomical body's atmosphere, especially affecting its surface, and strongly implying severe weather. It may be marked by strong wind, thunder and lightning (a thunderstorm), heavy precipitation, such as ice (ice storm), or wind transporting some substance through the atmosphere (as in a dust storm, snowstorm, hailstorm, etc).[1] Terry Lyles in his book, "The Secret to Navigating Life's Storms" has this to say about other storms that confront believers: "Life storms come in many forms: trauma, tragedy, illness, injury, depression, anxiety, financial reversal, divorce, and even the pressures and stress of day-to-day living."[2]

Living on the sin cursed earth incurs facing all sorts of perils. Storms are just one of them. Disaster struck New Orleans, one fateful morning. America was awakened up out of her deep spiritual slumber. God can bring great good from seeming bad. Wikipedia has these stunning fact about this disaster, "**Hurricane Katrina** of the 2005 Atlantic hurricane season was the costliest hurricane, as well as one of the five deadliest, in the history of the United States. It caused great damage to life and property especially in New Orleans. Frightful statistics by the same source reveal, "At least 1,836 people lost their lives in the actual hurricane and in the subsequent floods, making it the deadliest U.S. hurricane since the 1928 Okeechobee Hurricane. The storm is estimated to have been responsible for $81.2 billion (2005 U.S. dollars) in damage, making it the costliest tropical cyclone in U.S. history.[3] These statistics are scary, the numbers are huge.

Architects do consider these forces of nature, the possible threats of land and natural dangers when they build a house. Every home faces similar threats. Storms will test, try, and tear the home. The home must be well prepared to weather them. In my opinion storms are basically of two kinds. There are storms that confront a home from within, and there are also storms that confront the home from without.

The Bible warns, instructs, to guard the home against looming dangers. Every individual is totally depraved. Every human heart is desperately wicked. Most people trust the heart. They fail to understand its deceitfulness. Jesus warned of this deceptive heart. He said it is not the things we eat that defiles us, but the things that come out of our hearts. It is no wonder than that many attacks on the home come from within our own hearts. Mark 7: 21-22, enlists some sins arising from within the heart of man, "For from within, out of the heart of men, proceed evil thoughts, adulteries, fornications, murders, thefts, covetousness, wickedness, deceit, lasciviousness, an evil eye, blasphemy, pride, foolishness." These are sins that whelm up from within. These storms rage from the heart, birthing many storms in a home. God's Word issues warnings concerning these sins.

In the New Testament books of Ephesians (5: 22-33) and I Peter (3: 1-7) and Old Testament book of Proverbs (31), God carves out these instructions by divine inspiration. Jeremiah (17:9) speaks of the heart being desperately wicked. The heart is capable of committing terrible sins. Sins from within our hearts are deadly. They erupt causing untold damage to the home. They will wreck any marriage. In God's omniscience, He gave instructions by way of warning to each partner in a marital relationship. God lays out the roles each individual must play in a marriage. Permit me to list the roles and responsibilities. Here are a few Biblical principles that can be worked at from within. If these warnings are unheeded, they could shatter our homes. Hence, the Bible warns us. So, "Beware!"

STORMS THAT THREATEN THE HOME FROM WITHIN:

Each individual within the home must perform his/her role to the best of his/her ability. Each bears the responsibility to partner in this enormous project.

Partnering together helps bear the yoke of the home, share the burdens, and enjoy the blessings. Presented below are some of the God-given roles and responsibilities of the wife.

The Wife
- Is to submit to her own husband as unto the Lord (Eph. 5: 22)
- Is to be subject to her husband as the church is subject unto Christ (Eph. 5: 24)
- Is to reverence her husband (Eph. 5: 33)
- Is to be obedient (I Pet. 3: 1; Pro. 31: 5)
- Is to have a chaste conversation coupled with fear (I Pet. 3: 2)
- Is to adorn herself with a meek and quiet spirit (I Pet. 4)

- Is to trust God (I Pet. 3: 5)
- Is to be of value to the husband, more precious than rubies (Pro. 31: 10)
- Is able to make the heart of her husband to trust safely in her (Pro. 31: 11)
- Is to do him good (Pro. 31: 12)
- Is a willing worker (Pro. 31: 13)
- Is a hard worker providing for her family (Pro. 31: 15, 17)
- Is a woman that is industrious, making investments (Pro. 31: 16)
- Is a woman that plans (Pro. 31: 18)
- Is generous to the poor and needy (Pro. 31: 20)
- Is prepared to protect her home in any situation (Pro. 31: 21)
- Is a woman that carries a decent attire (Pro. 31: 22)
- Is a woman that gives her husband a good name and no reason to be ashamed (Pro. 31: 23)
- Is clothed with strength and honor (Pro. 31: 25)
- Is of a kind disposition (Pro. 31:26)
- Is never idle (Pro. 31: 27)
- Is praised by her children and husband (Pro. 31: 28)
- Is a woman that fears the Lord (31: 30)
- Is to be discreet (Titus 2: 5)
- Is to be chaste (v. 5)
- Is to be a keeper at home (v. 5)
- Is to be good (v. 5)

God's Word discloses the role the wife ought to play in a home. Submitting to her God-given role makes the home function the way God intended for it to function. The husband too has a role God wants him to play. He must fulfill his responsibilities. Obeying God brings blessings to the home. His responsibilities are outlined below.

The Husband
- Is the head of the wife as Christ is the head of the church (Eph. 5: 23)
- Is the savior of the body as Christ is the savior of the church (Eph. 5: 23)
- Is to love his own wife as Christ loved the church and gave himself for it (Eph. 5: 25)
- Is to love his own wife as his own body (Eph. 5: 28)
- Is to leave his father and mother (Eph. 5: 31)
- Is to cleave unto his wife (Eph. 5: 31)
- Is to become one flesh (Eph. 5: 31)
- Is to dwell with his wife (I Pet. 3: 7)
- Is to give honor unto his wife, as unto the weaker vessel (I Pet. 3: 7)
- Is to realize that they both together are heirs of the grace of life (I Pet. 3: 7)

When the husband and wife understand and abide by their God given roles and responsibilities, much of the internal storms of the home can be calmed, overcome or completely avoided. The contrary is true of those that disregard these roles. An unloving husband is harsh, unkind, and not a reflection of Christ. He fails to be a good leader. A leader must lead by example. Jesus compares the husband to Himself. Christ gave Himself for the church. He paid the ultimate price as an expression of His love. A man ought to, in like manner, be willing to make any sacrifice to express his love for his wife. Women are to be submissive to their own husbands. When women are not submissive, there is going to be a power struggle in the home. Children are confused as to who the real leader is. Their lives are messed up because their understanding of leadership is messed up. A wife with a meek and quiet spirit is beautiful, more beautiful than a woman that is beautiful externally. An outwardly beautiful woman can be ugly on the inside because of her boisterous disposition. The home will crumble from within when such tug-of-wars go on. Most homes expect storms from without, but, seldom anticipate storms from within. The devil uses each and every weapon in his armory to destroy the home. He looks for weak spots that are easy to penetrate. If he finds a weak link, he will destroy the home. The home is only as strong as its weakest link.

Submission does not mean keeping quiet or silent for everything. It means working in harmony while performing the God given role. God took Eve from Adam's side, so she could be his helpmeet, not a foot stool. Our present world promotes women to fight for their rights. The younger generation of women is taught they are to have equal rights. This upsets the God given pattern for the establishment of the home so it can function harmoniously. God knows, for a home to function well, there ought to be order. Order is essential in every area of life. Where there is no order, there is confusion. Where there is no order, there is no beauty. A symphony is a perfect illustration of this truth. So many instruments are involved in an orchestra. If every musician played his own tune, without synchronizing with the others musicians in the orchestra, the music wouldn't be pleasant to the ear. It would be just a whole lot of noise. But, when each musician plays his part, the music becomes enjoyable. To make all the musicians play in synch or in harmony there ought to be a music director. He is the leader to orchestrate the musicians, to oversee that no one is messing up. In order for the home to function smoothly, God has established order. He made the husband the head of the home. The wife is to help him perform his God-given role. Children become part of this home. Once they are added they must align themselves to perform their responsibilities. Working women have brought a whole new ball game to the table. Many problems arise because of two earning members. Issues of control over money, decisions, and roles at home have all become a challenge instead of being a pleasure. All this has come about because of failure to understand one's God-given role.

Women who do not comprehend their role try to dominate or control their husbands. Barbara Butler Norrell, while trying to control her husband writes these words of caution, "I fell in love with

Larry exactly as he was. Yet, it seemed that as soon as I'd fallen in love, I started taking advantage of him. This is scary, it's like the more love a woman feels for someone, the more we actually start taking things for granted and wanting to change him."[4] Control extends not only to being authoritative but spreads to many other areas of life. Notice her confession, "I can change your hair...let's see, if you comb your hair back and put some gel in it, it would take years off your face. Honey, if you wear jeans, you'll look ten years younger.[5] Control could extend to, even as far as, into the bed room, affecting intimacy. "I also realize that women can be tempted to control their husbands by using sex as a means of reward or punishment. This is unscriptural, but more than this, it's just plain wrong-because it's taking advantage of someone you love."[6]

I proposed to Leah in November, 1993, was engaged in March, 1994, and I got married to her in May that same year. My life changed drastically during these six months. Six months earlier, I was a bachelor, but now, a married man. Many big adjustments had to be made. I praise God for the godly parents Leah had. Leah's dad was my spiritual father. He gave us precious advice. During our courtship time, he said, "Lee and Richy, don't put on a mask. Be honest and expose your weaknesses. Talk openly to each other about everything." I did love his advice. Tell me, which man likes to expose all his weaknesses and does not try to impress his fiancée? I was all out to impress her, thinking in my mind, "I am your prince charming. I am the man of your dreams. I have all that you are looking for in a man." I did not want to blemish her expectation of me, nor tarnish my reputation.

During my courtship days I had permission to meet with Leah twice a week. Her parents had many rules laid out for us. We could meet at her house, in the living room, where everyone could see us. This was good, a boundary that helped keep our courtship pure. I was allotted an hour of time that I could spend on each visit. I wasn't going to waste these precious minutes with her relating all my flaws. Do you think I was going to tell her, "I have a problem with selfishness?" Was I going to tell her I did get angry sometimes. Now, I wish we had a longer courtship, so we both could have had the time to see both sides of our character. These exposures are not meant to bring our expectations down, rather they would have helped us see what hurdles lay ahead. We could have prayed or sought God's help to tackle them. Though, I did not take full advantage of my courtship to expose my weakness, God was faithful. God helped me deal with these issues during my early years of marriage. We did spend time in prayer. We did establish our home on the right foundation. We did ensure we erected the right pillars to support our home. This did not mean the storms were well past. They would strike us, time and again.

During the early stages of our new home, many storms struck us from within. Leah and I were totally different. We had such contrasting temperaments. We had our own likes and dislikes. Acclimating ourselves to each other was hard enough. Yet, many new battles had to be faced as well. Battles involving: selfishness, anger, tiredness, procrastination, and playing the blame game. Looking back, I see how God transformed us more through all of these skirmishes, into His glorious image. I did not like going through these conflicts at that time, even though God had a plan, a reason for why He allowed them in my life.

Trials ripped my home, exposing my true inner character. Every time I was pulled up for something, I felt as if the whole world was watching me. I felt like the whole world was against me. I was being made a spectacle. I pitied myself, saying, "Poor me." I even gave myself a pat on the back. Told myself, "You're not as bad as they are making you feel." Get the picture? Now I know I am not all good or all bad. I must admit, I was a sinner, simply saved by grace. I need grace each day. Grace so God can work on me for the rest of my life. Grace to be transformed into God's glorious image.

We must realize, however, there are storms that strike from within. I did not want to be the problem; I want to be the solution. The Bible says in Matthew (Mt 18:7), "Woe unto the world because of offences! for it must needs be that offences come; but woe to that man by whom the offence cometh!" I simply did not want to be the problem, be it in the home, my job, my church or elsewhere. My prayer, "Dear Lord, help me not to cause offenses." Though, this is always my prayer, my nature did offend some. Over time I have learned to be more careful. I still need to grow in this area; there is a long way to go. Thanks be to God, He has not given up on me. He is still working on me. He speaks to my heart. I am yielding to His directive voice.

External storms strike from without. Examining the Bible reveals the existence of internal storms, but there are external storms as well. It's time to examine and expose them. They must be identified, wrestled with, or even snuffed out until with God's help we can have consistent victories over them.

STORMS THAT THREATEN THE HOME FROM WITHOUT

Paul teaches believers some valuable lessons about the home. He provides priceless insights into the relationships that exist within. I Corinthians chapter seven talks a lot about some do's and don'ts. Other passages in Proverbs 6 and II Timothy 3 provide help to strengthen the home. He enlists some of these dangers:

- The threat: of committing Fornication (7: 2)
  Sexual relationships outside the bounds of marriage are detrimental to the establishing of a strong home.
- The threat from either partner: not to defraud one another of intimacy in marriage (7: 3-5)
  Lack of intimacy in marriage will drive a partner to seek intimacy from someone else outside of marital boundaries. Paul warns of this danger.

- The threat of temptation: to divorce for any reason (7: 10)

    Small untended frictions will become big in time. A proverb says, "A stitch in time saves nine." Lubricate your relationship with the oil of communication. Many problems can be easily solved or dissolved by simply communicating. Beware of the "little foxes" that spoil the vine (Song of Solomon 2: 15).

- The threat to divorce: is not permissible till either one partner dies (v. 39)

    God's desire and design for individuals that partner in the making of a home, is for an entire lifetime. God wants the relationship to be between one man and one woman only. Marital relationship ends only when either partner dies. This is God's way, the Bible way.

- The threat of being unequally yoked: in marriages (one partner not saved, v. 11)

    Being unequally yoked means choosing a partner that is unsaved. Partnering with an unsaved person in marriage or for business ventures will almost always end in heartache. Believers are to separate from the world. An unequal yoke makes it impossible for both partners to have the same goals, visions and worship.

- The threat to lust after the evil woman (Pro. 6: 24)

    A man is warned to stay far from an evil woman. He must flee her presence. She is a trap, he will ultimately fall prey to her. The lures she uses include: flattery, her natural beauty, and her looks (neither let her take thee with her eyelids). Proverbs 6:26-28 warns of the detrimental results produced on the man trapped by her, "For by means of a whorish woman a man is brought to a piece of bread: and the adulteress will hunt for the precious life. Can a man take fire in his bosom, and his clothes not be burned? Can one go upon hot coals, and his feet not be burned?"

She is a fire that will consume him, setting him spiraling on a downward path of destruction.

- The threat against apostasy (II Tim. 3: 1-7)

The threat against apostasy threatens the home. Paul warns of apostasy. In context of the home, apostasy is a sin of loving that which is unnatural. Satan dangles apostasy before people eyes, as bait before a fish. In Paul's day, during a time when the Church was in its baby stage, this threat was real. It remains a grave a threat in our day. Thus Paul warns the saints (II Tim. 3: 1-7),

This know also, that in the last days perilous times come.
For men shall be lovers of their own selves, covetous, disobedient to parents, unthankful, unholy,
Without natural affection, trucebreakers, false accusers, incontinent, fierce, despisers of those that are good,
Traitors, heady, highminded, lovers of pleasure more than lovers of God.
Having a form of godliness, but denying the power thereof: from such turn away.

> For of this sort are they **which creep into houses**, and lead captive silly women laden with sins, led away with divers lusts,
>
> Ever learning, and never able to come to the knowledge of the truth.

Grave dangers threaten the home. Homosexualities,and lesbianism, pose an ever-increasing threat, especially as the end-time approaches. Paul's letter to Timothy warns women to be careful, to beware of these creepy hazards for they find a way of sneaking into the home. Satan realizes women are weaker vessels. He targets them to get into the home and wedges his way in, trying to tear it down.

Other dangers enter the home through external sources. Listed below and explained briefly are a few modern-day threats.

TELEVISION MEDIA

Modern media has brought sin right into our homes, making these sins available and accessible. Fornication is not considered sin any more. People believe it is a way of life. Some chose to live life that way. They say, "It is my choice and entirely upto me, to live the way I like." Values and morals are depreciating each day. Governments make laws promoting these values, all in the name of 'discrimination.'

Television, while can be very useful, is becoming a creepy tool the devil is using to infiltrate our homes. Through it, he promotes mixed marriages, homosexuality, lesbianism, bad language, vulgar dressing, and ungodly music. These sins are only the tip of the iceberg of problems modern-day media presents. The television is used extensively to promote wrong philosophies. It has become a marketing tool for anything and everything. Tele-evangelists are taking advantage of this form of media. Some teach truth, while others distort truth. Many are teaching false doctrines. Many innocent and ignorant Christians fall prey to these men who promise to be God's messengers. They are wolves in sheep's clothing. We must be aware of these dangers. We must be careful to study God's Word to be able to discern the right from the wrong. The home must be guarded against things that creep in unawares.

COMPUTERS AND INTERNET

Computers have become almost indispensable these days. They have become a necessity. Almost every home has a computer today. Even third world countries have seen and do know a great deal about computers. The world has become a closer unit from the time they have arrived. E-mail and chat have made it possible to communicate at lightning speed. The days of the foot-running mail man have faded into the distant past. A total transformation has taken place in communication. As is the case with all technology, each new gadget has both positive and negative uses.

With these technological advantages, also come other real dangers that threaten to skulk the home. These threats invade our homes. They come from the outside world. Wikipedia provides a statistic of how quickly computers are finding their way into most homes, the world over.

> In 2001 125 <u>million</u> personal computers were shipped in comparison to 48 <u>thousand</u> in 1977. More than 500 million PCs were in use in 2002 and one <u>billion</u> personal computers had been sold worldwide since mid-1970s till this time. Of the latter figure, 75 percent were professional or work related, while the rest sold for personal or home use. About 81.5 percent of PCs shipped had been <u>desktop computers</u>, 16.4 percent <u>laptops</u> and 2.1 percent <u>servers</u>. United States had received 38.8 percent (394 million) of the computers shipped, Europe 25 percent and 11.7 percent had gone to Asia-Pacific region, the fastest-growing market as of 2002. The second billion was expected to be sold by 2008.[2] Almost half of all the households in <u>Western Europe</u> had a personal computer and a computer could be found in 40 percent of homes in United Kingdom, compared with only 13 percent in 1985.[3]
>
> As of June 2008, the number of personal computers in use worldwide hit one billion, while another billion is expected to be reached by 2014. Mature markets like the United States, <u>Western Europe</u> and Japan accounted for 58 percent of the worldwide installed PCs. The <u>emerging markets</u> were expected to double their installed PCs by 2013 and to take 70 percent of the second billion PCs.⁷

The devil is using this form of media to enter our homes. More people can get access to a computer with each passing day, even if they do not own one. Many wicked things are displayed, advertised and sold through the computer. Many bad massages are delivered to our door steps via the email. Bad song videos and other vulgar material flash to gain our attention. They are literally a mouse click away. Bringing computers into our home have many pros and cons. The cons are the ones we must worry about. These are real dangers. They pose a high level of danger because they can be viewed in secret. While computers have many wonderful uses, the bad seems to outweigh the good. Another media proves to be a menace and threat to our homes and our kids. This treat is the media of modern-day music.

MUSIC MEDIA

Worldly music is another danger that enters our sensory gates. Bad music is everywhere. The lyrics of music in plain audios or videos cause the heart to desire forbidden fruit. Ungodly songs are used by Satan to lure more people into his trap. He offers a new kind of spirituality. Believers are to live in the world but are not to be part of the worldly system. Satan knows believers are aware of these truths. Thus, he is using so-called godly songs, even godly lyrics to bring the world into the church. He does not mind spiritual lyrics, but he gives those lyrics worldly beat. This makes the church no different from a club. Our younger generation is attracted to this modern church. The devil is a master of disguise. He is a deceiver. Back at the beginning of creation, he deceived Eve into believing his lie. People have grown to accept such seemingly spiritual songs, sung by unbelieving artists, with open arms. Guard your ear gate.

Pastors are drifting away from the Bible. Poor church attendance has made preachers desperate. Rather than trying to seek God's help to build the church, they use human wisdom. This is disastrous. Human wisdom tells them to seek human methods. In perusing this method they believe, "It's ok to add some fizz to the music. Old music is dull and boring, anyway." Human wisdom is contrary to God's methods. Human wisdom displays selfishness, pride, and total independence from God. God wants us to depend on Him.

Some pastors believe worldly methods will probably work to their benefit and aid them to increase their numbers; invite the world into their pews for the wrong reasons. When they invite worldly people into the church by using worldly methods, they are now forced to satisfy them with worldly means. Having drawn a worldly, unsaved crowd, they believe they can now indoctrinate them with spiritual things. This is a mega failure, a truly false notion. We must be careful not to use worldly methods for spiritual purposes. This is abomination. Our homes cannot be holy ground if we let these modern philosophies creep into our home.

Modern technology has made it both attractive and available for our children to own an IPod or an MP3 player. Though these gadgets are useful they can also be misused. Most electronic companies are targeting the younger generation. They make youngsters believe their products are "cool." They convincingly advertise saying, "It's sleek, easy to use, and that it makes a fashion statement." Guard your children from these trends that flow as horrendous currents or whirlpools. Currents deceive. Though they appear calm on the surface, beneath the current, the reality is quite different. Those trapped in the current find it hard to escape its grip. They will be sucked in. Currents are terribly destructive. Heed the warning, "Warning!" Warnings are posted everywhere. They flash like bright red lights in the verses of Scripture issuing warnings. One such warning is issued in the book of I Peter 5:8, "Be sober, be vigilant; because your adversary the devil, as a roaring lion, walketh about, seeking whom he may devour:" Guard your home. Guard your heart from this creepy destroyer.

MAGAZINES MEDIA

Newspaper and magazines pose a serious threat. Magazines are everywhere. They turn the hearts of people from the foundational principles of God's Holy Word. Their extensive availability makes them readily available in grocery stores. They can be bought from a vending machine on the street. Bad pictures span the pages. Worldly advice fills its every line. We must flee from this kind of duress's. No one is strong enough to fight them on their own. They attract our attention by appealing to the flesh gaining access through the eye gate. We must be careful not to fall a prey. We must not let it intimidate us. We need God's help to conquer this enemy. It may be impossible to avoid seeing magazines everywhere we go, but we must be careful to turn our eyes away from the vile images displayed on its covers. Our thoughts are never to dwell on evil things. I paraphrase a quotation I heard illustrated betimes, "Let the birds fly over our heads, but never let them build nests on our heads." I am uncertain who the author is, however, it is a wonderful thought. Dwelling on evil, produces evil. Paul admonishes believers to think on things he lists to edify in Phil. 4: 8, "Finally, brethren, whatsoever things are true, whatsoever things are honest, whatsoever things are just, whatsoever things are pure, whatsoever things are lovely, whatsoever things are of good report; if there be any virtue, and if there be any praise, think on these things."

LEARNING FROM THE PAST

JOSEPH'S JEOPARDY

Jacob's family met with storms from both within and without. Jacob loved Joseph dearly. Joseph's brother's hated him for that very fact. They sold him. When in Egypt, Potipher's wife had him sent to jail, falsely accusing him of seducing her. Innocent, yet punished, he spent two long years in a prison cell. Yet for all, you never find him grumbling, murmuring, complaining or whining. Joseph's trials (in the Old Testament) did not make him bitter. They made him better. When the world saw his life as a series of disasters, he saw the determinative hand of God crafting him into an object of beauty. His brothers meant it all for evil, but God meant it for good.

JOB'S TRIALS AND TRIUMPHS

God turned Job's trials into triumphs. Job went through some turbulent times in his life. His story in the Bible begins by describing his great strength of character. He was blessed with great riches. He had seven sons and three daughters. He owned, seven thousand sheep; three thousand camels, five hundred yoke of oxen, and five hundred she asses. Job evidently had established a good home. He was a godly man, feared God and was upright. He shunned evil.

Job's happy life was about to experience some horrendous situations. His nice life was about to become a nightmare. His trouble-free life was about to turn turbulent. One beautiful, bright day of his life, would turn dark, dreadful, disastrous in just a few hours. A messenger came running up to him. As on any other day of his life, Job thought it probably was not going to be a message too alarming. This day would be different. It would shock him out of his skin. It would wobble him out of his wits. He brought bad news saying (Job 1: 14b-15), "The oxen were plowing, and the asses feeding beside them: And the Sabeans fell upon them, and took them away; yea, they have slain the servants with the edge of the sword; and I only am escaped alone to tell thee." Another common proverb goes like this, "when it rains it pours." A true statement in Job's life. Tragedy after tragedy struck his home. Next, while the servant was yet speaking, another messenger brought gloomy news (Job 1: 16b-17), "The fire of God is fallen from heaven, and hath burned up the sheep, and the servants, and consumed them; and I only am escaped alone to tell thee."

Another messenger arrived in quick succession, panting, conveying a message while the former was yet speaking. He says (1:

17b-17f), "The Chaldeans made out three bands, and fell upon the camels, and have carried them away, yea, and slain the servants, with the edge of the sword; and I only am escaped alone to tell thee." In much the same fashion one last messenger came dashing with more heartbreaking news (1: 18b-19), "Thy sons and thy daughters were eating and drinking wine in their eldest brother's house. And behold, there came a great wind from the wilderness and smote the four corners of the house, and it fell upon the young men, and they are dead; and I only am escaped alone to tell thee."

All that Job had, was now gone. The events of Job's life on that day rocked his world. It is hard to imagine the feelings Job experienced that day, in a short span of time. His "Riches to rags" story probably made headlines on every newspaper cover. He became the talk of the town. Broken in heart, soul and spirit, he rent his mantel, shaved his head and fell down upon the ground. Wrenched of his every energy Job finds strength to draw one staggering conclusion in 23:10, "But he knoweth the way that I take: when He hath tried me, I shall come forth as gold." The last word of verse twenty reveals the key to his success in weathering storms. Despite his calamity, Job found in himself the strength to "worship" God. His victory came because he never lost focus on God. He kept his eye on God. Even though Job lost all, he had not lost his all, for he still had his all in God. His home crumbled, but his foundations stood strong. He was rooted and grounded in God.

Why The Home Crumbles

Fifteen years have gone by since I got married. Leah and I have faced many trials, oppositions, hurricanes, tornadoes, even some very rough storms of life. Our home could have come crashing down. Our castle could have been ripped apart. Many situations did bring us to the brink of throwing in the towel. I wanted to quit. We wanted to quit. I heard this statement sometime in my life. It captured my attention. I don't know who said it but it stayed in my mind. The statement says, "Winners never quit and quitters never win."

The statement stuck in my mind. I, realized, "Jesus, my Lord is a Victor." If this is true, I can't quit. In Christ, we are more than conquerors. He is my strength. I can go on. The lyrics of a Sunday school song helps smile instead of scowl. It reads, "With Christ in my vessel I can smile at the storm." We remember: some long, dark nights; some tearful days; some painful memories; some heavy hearted days but how we thank God for Jesus. The words of this song seem to fit my life's struggles well,

> I've had many tears and sorrows,
> I've had questions for tomorrow,
> There've been times I didn't know right from wrong:
> But in every situation God gave blessed consolation
> That my trials come to only make me strong.
>
> Through it all, through it all,
> I've learned to trust in Jesus,
> I've learned to trust in God;
> Through it all, through it all,
> I've learned to depend upon His Word.

> I've been to lots of places,
> And I've seen a lot of faces,
> There've been times I felt so all alone;
> But in my lonely hours,
> Yes, those precious lonely hours,
> Jesus let me know that I was His own.
>
> Through it all, through it all,
> I've learned to trust in Jesus,
> I've learned to trust in God;
> Through it all, through it all,
> I've learned to depend upon His Word.
>
> I thank God for the mountains,
> And I thank Him for the valleys,
> I thank Him for the storms
> He brought me through;
> For if I'd never had a problem
> I wouldn't know that He could solve them,
> I'd never know what faith in God could do.
>
> Through it all, through it all,
> I've learned to trust in Jesus,
> I've learned to trust in God;
> Through it all, through it all,
> I've learned to depend upon His Word.[8]

Discouragement came from within the family and without. Determining to lay a firm foundation, determining to involve God in everything we did, made our home withstand the storms of life. We were determined to have God in our vessel. Leah and I purposed to have God as our foundation. We choose to let God help us build our home. The glory belongs to God, for every victory we have enjoyed. It is all because of Him I made it thus far. Job's endurance is well worth reflecting upon for one last time in this chapter. Job had endured much. His pain was very grievous indeed. He had suffered so much loss. He lost his: home and happiness, his family and friends and even his possessions and posterity. He lost financially and physically. When his turmoil was almost ended, all that was left was Job and his wife. From the pinnacle of his position as one of the leaders who sat at the city gates, to the world he looked pitiful sitting upon a heap of ashes. God was doing a work in His life. It would make him more wonderful than before. He just did not know that yet.

Paul the apostle of Jesus Christ suffered many a loss in his life, but he remained undefeated. He writes (I Cor. 4: 11-13), "Even unto this present hour we both hunger, and thirst, and are naked, and are buffeted, and have no certain dwellingplace; And labour, working with our own hands:" He did go through the fire. Do you think he cried or complained? He could well have justified responding in such a manner, but he continued to joyfully pen down his pain, "Being reviled, we bless; being persecuted, we suffer it: Being defamed, we intreat: we are made as the filth of the world, and are the offscouring of all things unto this day.

Job suffered unbearable physical pain. Petrifying sores, boils covered his entire body. So painful were the sores, he took a potsherd to scrape himself while sitting amongst ashes. His worst nightmare confronted him, when his dear wife uttered words he wished never came from her mouth (Job 2: 9), "Dost thou still retain thine integrity? cruse God, and die." Job response is gallant. He had the nerve to respond to her suggestion, with these words, (2: 10), "But he said unto her, Thou speakest as one of the foolish women speaketh. What? shall we receive good at the hand of God and shall we not receive evil. In all this did not Job sin with his lips." Some of his friends forsook him, others tormented him with piercing words. Amongst them he found no comforters. Without much ado, let me conclude, Job saw a silver lining right through his dark, dreadfully, black, seemingly impenetrable thick cloud. When his earthly reasoning read zero visibility, his spiritual perception was clear. Mustering up courage, he said (Job 23: 10) "But he knoweth the way that I take: when he hath tried me, I shall come forth as gold."

Can you weather the storms of life that threaten your home? Yes you can! With God as your foundation, you surely can. Job's story ends wonderfully well. Job 42: 12-13 lays the capstone to his story, "So the LORD blessed the latter end of Job more than his beginning: for he had fourteen thousand sheep, and six thousand camels, and a thousand yoke of oxen, and a thousand she asses. He had also seven sons and three daughters." His resolve to encompass God in his blue print, plan, foundation, and home made him victorious. I ask you again; Can your home weather storms? YES, YOUR HOME CAN!

GOD'S HELP LINE

Which family or individual does not need help? Every human goes through stressful situations in life. Oft-times situations seem to surge out of control. Man must see he is finite by nature, a mere creature. Every creature needs help during turbulent times. Men need the help of their Creator, God. We often fail to acknowledge we need help. He alone knows our composition. God has given to us a two-way line of communication. He has given us His Word so we can hear His voice, heed His direction, and satisfy His expectations. On the other hand, God has given us the ability to pray, an opportunity for man to commune with God. Unlike phone lines that fail to work in an earthquake, or natural disaster, God's lines of communication never crash. They work 24/7, 365 days of year, never a moment when you will find a busy tone.

We need God's help if we want to warranty success while building our homes. He is the chief architect of the home. If so, when we find ourselves at crossroads, or facing unassailable obstacles, we need to find out His ideas, His solutions and His answers to our queries. For He alone has the blue print. He wrote the manual. Prayer makes communication possible. "Seek the LORD and his strength, seek his face continually" is the suggestion given in I Chronicles (16:11). Valuable advice indeed! Consistent prayer assures of consistent progress in building our home.

Especially in poor countries, builders often expect the unexpected. Building projects may face dead ends. Finances may run out. There may be a lack of workers because of this. Building materials may not be available on time. There may be a delay in getting appropriate materials transported. Likewise, building the home has its own set of difficulties. There is no need for panic. There's help. Help is available round the clock. Believers will not find themselves outside of customer service hours. We don't have to listen to tiresome, heartless message on the answering machine. We can reach God, the divine architect directly and immediately, with success. There will be no busy tone or an answer that says, "The person you are now trying to reach is unavailable, please call later," or these words, "If you like to leave a voice message, please press one and after you have recorded your message, please press pound."

You don't need to dial 9-1-1 to get on the emergency line to call God, to get his help. He will readily answer, (Ps 145:18-19), "The LORD is nigh unto all them that call upon him, to all that call upon him in truth. He will fulfill the desire of them that fear him: he also will hear their cry, and will save them." How blest to know you can reach God anytime, from anywhere.

No problem is too big for God to handle. No mountain too high that He cannot climb. No catastrophe too big or out of His control. Nothing He cannot mend. He is a master fixer. He can fix broken homes, broken lives and broken hearts. God can. He alone can! God wants our homes to succeed. He wants us to heed His Word. He wants us to seek His counsel. What hinders us from seeking His help? Why are we shy to go to His presence? He wants us to depend on Him. God wants us to express confidence in Him. He says (Matt 21:22), "And all things, whatsoever ye shall ask in prayer, believing, ye shall receive." Isn't this blessed assurance? Now that we have such confidence in our Almighty God, we can weather the storms of life. We know we can build homes that last. But the question, what are we going to leave behind? What kind of a legacy will we leave? Think about it.

CHAPTER SEVEN

CAUTION! WHAT ARE WE BUILDING? WHAT ARE WE LEAVING BEHIND?

Excitement was in the air. Enthusiasm was welling up within me. First, my bachelor days came to an end. Life had me meander through various stages. I had the wonderful joy of being a son, a brother, a student, a faculty at Calvary Baptist Bible College and Seminary (11 years) and a pastor at Whitefield Baptist Church (11 years). As an adult, my life took new turns. I became a husband to Leah. Until my marriage, I had lived for my parents and brothers. Having started a home, I had a new God-given role to fulfill. I was a husband. Soon, I was going to become a brand new father.

Many thoughts paced through my mind. All my life flashed before me as a dream. I thought about my childhood, my teenage years, and now I was a man. Life seemed to have quickly passed me by. I was entering a new phase in life. Fatherhood seemed to be an enormous responsibility. I did not know how I would face or handle it.

OUR NEW ARRIVAL

As the time for our first baby's arrival drew near, Leah had to make periodical doctor's visits. On one visit, the doctor ordered an ultrasound scan. The results brought mixed news. "Let me give you the good news first," the doctor said, "your baby is doing fine." Then she continued on to reveal the bad news, "your baby cannot be delivered normally because there are loops of cords around the neck." I looked at Leah for I did not understand what the doctor said. I sensed though, the news couldn't be too good for Leah's eyes flooded with tears. We had prayed for her to have a normal delivery since the time she conceived. Though the thought of this was depressing, it brought mixed feelings, yet, the joy of having our first baby brought great exhilaration.

The doctor gave us very little choice. We had to pick a day (within the next two days) and admit Leah into the (Church of South India Hospital, Bangalore, India) hospital for a C-Section. In November, 1995, our first son Gideon was born. Just the joy of having a normal, healthy baby boy brought so much happiness. We soon forgot the surgery and the emotional pain. God was good. God is always good. He knows "best" what was going on. He knows "why" He allowed the situation. We did not need to despair because God is always in control. I do admit as a human, I did feel some fear. I had learned theoretically to turn all my cares to prayers, but putting it into practice was a totally different story. It still is.

Fatherhood seemed quite awkward at first. I was thrilled to be a dad. I did not know how to behave. I saw this little baby lying near Leah. I had never handled a baby so small. It took a while for me to get used to this new role. Many strange feelings and thoughts flashed across my mind. The joy was immeasurable. Soon, an overwhelming sense of responsibility flooded my soul. God had entrusted another life in my hands. Together, we had to bring up this little baby in the nurture and admonition of the Lord.

OVERWHELMING FACTS

Children are not born by accident. Though God gave man the ability to procreate, yet God had to initiate life, give form and fashion the baby in the mother's womb. From conception to birth, the journey of the sperm is an extraordinary one. When the sperm meets the egg, the fetus is formed. The next forty weeks brought about the transformation of this little life form, from fetus to a full-grown baby is nothing short of a wonderful miracle. The Bible declares (Psalm 139: 14-15), "I will praise thee; for I am fearfully and wonderfully made: marvelous are thy works; and that my soul knoweth right well. My substance was not hid from thee, when I was made in secret, and curiously wrought in the lowest parts of the earth." David is amazed, just like I was, at God's involvement in the creation of a baby.

God took time to form every bone, every muscle, every organ, had even worked on every minute detail. David spoke of God's intricate designing of his body in Psalm 139:16-18. In verse 16 he mentions, "Thine eyes did see my substance, yet being imperfect; and in thy book all my members were written, which in continuance were fashioned, when as yet there was none of them." He continues to describe God's intentions in taking time to design every man (vv.17-18), "How precious also are thy thoughts unto me, O God! how great is the sum of them! If I should count them, they are more in number than the sand: when I awake, I am still with thee." As a child, I felt very insecure. Many reasons caused me to be the timid person that I was. I felt less of a person, somewhat less capable of doing things in comparison to my brothers. These feelings did not elude me after I entered the ministry. However, things did change when I joined Bible College. God began to work in me. I found new verses in the Bible though they were in existence for centuries. These were days of new discoveries for me. These verses proved to be spiritual gold mines, pillars of strength, strengthening my faith. Oft times, I had come to the end of the road, in my life. I decided, it was enough, I could not take it anymore. I determined to end it all. I weighed the decision to call it "quits."

Difficult days made me feel like I was losing control. Failures in my life almost proved fatal. Nevertheless, God had a plan, a better plan. He enabled me to go through these situations. When I first read Psalm 139, it was like water to a man stranded and dying in a burning-hot desert. I was not a failure, a flaw or a fatality, but the result of God's intricate design. Negativity was all I saw when I looked inward. Pessimism can spiral a person downward out of control. It sucks you like a whirlpool into the depths of despair. Looking upward is the only way out. It is the only secret key which can unlocks anyone from such a situation. Looking upward to God was the way I found strength to soar through all of life's difficulties. He alone could help me out of all my misery. I stopped being negative about myself. I decided to crucify my self-pitying, all those terrible feelings of inferiority. I did not see myself as a useless person anymore. I saw, I was uniquely designed by God. I am the result of His design, His plan. God fashioned me from my mother's womb. Another Bible verse affirms this truth (Psalm 119: 73), "Thy hands have made me and fashioned me." A fresh, godly attitude made me see things differently. Any complaint, petulance or murmur was an accusation directly pointed at God. I did not want to accuse God, my creator. Looking upward enabled me to look outward rather than inward. Looking to God took selfishness out of the equation. It got things in the right perspective. Reaching to meet the needs of others took the focus of me. It brought joy. Now, I am so thankful for who I am. I am God's design.

Paul writes in the book of 1 Cor. 15:10, "But by the grace of God I am what I am." Just the thought of being alive, the thought that I am a chosen vessel makes me a thankful person. God chose to save me. He chose to use me by calling me into the ministry. It is such an honor to be chosen, to serve the true and living God. I realize I don't deserve to be called by the Almighty God. It is by His grace I am a choice vessel. How fortunate to serve the true and living God. I really am so fortunate. I shouldn't say 'fortunate'. I reckon, "I am blessed." That's the right word, "Blessed." Yes! How blessed I really am! Praise God!" Now, I live to fulfill God's plan and purpose for my life. There is nothing more satisfying in the entire world, I assure you. Will you do the same?

OUR GARGANTUAN RESPONSIBILITY

The husband and wife are all it takes to have a home. Children are added to it. Never forget, the husband-wife relationship is the most important. It must always be first. Never let children run a home. A home run by children is headed towards ruin. God's design of the home is unique. It has a place for everyone. Each individual in the home has a position, a role to perform.

Children come into a home. They are a big blessing, never a burden. Psalm 127: 3 states, "Lo, children are an heritage of the LORD: and the fruit of the womb is his reward." Children are an inheritance from the Lord. They are God's gift to a family. Rearing them for God is a serious responsibility. God has lent them to us, to have, to hold, and to enjoy for a time. We are to return them to the Lord in due time. We are accountable for the way we treat, train and temper them. Children are our heritage. Nothing on earth is of more value, in this transient world, than our children. Remember to keep the priorities right. God must be first in everything.

Earthly treasures form a temporal part of our lives. They may come and go. The Bible says (Pro. 23: 5), Wilt thou set thine eyes upon that which is not? for riches certainly make themselves wings; they fly away as an eagle toward heaven." Riches do not guarantee happiness. You can buy the best water bed but it can never buy you sleep. Riches have their limitations. There are many things money cannot buy. It cannot buy salvation, joy, peace, love, friendship and a whole lot more. Money attracts people for the wrong reasons. People don't love you for who you are, but for the riches you possess. Money can allow you to host a party but it can never buy you true friends.

Money can buy medicine but not health. In my little village called "Whitefield", back home in Bangalore city in India, is a very prosperous cloth merchant. On one occasion when my mom was at his store to make a purchase, they got into a conversation about his sick mother. My mother narrated his story to me. He said to her, "Mrs. Jacob, my mother is dying of cancer. I am willing to pay any amount of money to get her cured, but the doctor said he cannot save her life." All the money he possessed could not save his dying mother.

Money can buy you a house, but never a home. Many rich people's homes are broken. They have everything money could possibly buy, yet their homes are tragically shattered. Too many people have their thinking distorted. They believe getting rich is the answer to all their problems. This is a terribly deceptive notion. Money can buy medicine but not health. This statement is so true.

My grandpa, Cyril Alfred Parker was a wealthy man. He had 24 acres of land, a big house and many comforts. He owned a car in the early 1920's (in India). My grandma was a sickly person. She had severe asthma. He spent most of his money taking care of his beloved wife, loving her dearly. Within his lifetime, he lost all his wealth, catering to her needs. I saw how much he loved her, even in his old age. He lovingly did things to see her happy. I thank God for an exemplary grandfather I was so privileged to have. The Bible is true. Riches do take wings and fly away. Unlike stories of people that rose from "rags to riches,' my grandfather's story was one, quite the opposite. His story spiraled down from "riches to rags." Oft, I heard my grandfather repeat for some reason (Mark 8:36), "For what shall it profit a man, if he shall gain the whole world, and lose his own soul?" I guess he understood from his personal experience how riches do take wings and fly away. He understood the importance of salvation of the soul in comparison to fleeting riches of this transient life.

OUR RICH HERITAGE

A heritage is something that we pass down. In the book "Your Heritage", J. Otis Ledbetter and Kurt Bruner define heritage as, "A heritage is the spiritual, emotional, and social legacy that is passed from parent to child....good or bad."[1] I would like to add one more statement to this neat definition. I would like to define the word "heritage" in my own words giving it a spiritual dimension. So, let me redefine it. I believe "heritage" is the passing down of our godly possessions from generation to generation, until Christ comes back to take us home. The word "godly" in my definition refers to a package deal. I will explain this as we progress in this study.

Many people lay up earthly treasures for their children or even for their children's children. This is not a bad idea. However, in comparison to what the Bible has to say about laying up of earthly treasures, we may want to re-evaluate that idea. The Bible says, (Matt 6:19-20), "Lay not up for yourselves treasures upon earth, where moth and rust doth corrupt, and where thieves break through and steal: But lay up for yourselves treasures in heaven, where neither moth nor rust doth corrupt, and where thieves do not break through nor steal." We are to lay up treasures in God's eternal bank. The treasures we store here on earth below: will take wings; will be fuel for fire one day; and will be consumed like a moth flying into a fire. The moth is attracted to light and heat. This thought makes me ponder more earnestly about my savings. How big a bank balance do I have in "The Bank of Heaven?" What is my present bank balance in God's eternal bank? What kind of investment must I make here on earth to store up great treasures in heaven, treasure which will not corrupt? Seeds for thought indeed!

Another book in the New Testament speaks of our inheritance, an inheritance incorruptible by nature. I Peter (1:3-4) tells us, "Blessed be the God and Father of our Lord Jesus Christ, which according to his abundant mercy hath begotten us again unto a lively hope by the resurrection of Jesus Christ from the dead, To an inheritance incorruptible, and undefiled, and that fadeth not away, reserved in heaven for you." Salvation is one incorruptible treasure the believer can never lose. We should make sure our family knows the Lord. Having this assurance provides security. It is an incorruptible inheritance we can store up in heaven's bank. Next, make wise investments so you can have a big bank balance in heaven's eternal bank.

DOWN MEMORY LANE

GIGLY GIDEON

Going back to the story of our first child brings me to a place of some sobering realities. The birth of a child is a wonderful occasion to celebrate. Gideon's birth brought great joy. It was a thrilling experience. I did not know how to control my emotions. I was ecstatic. We bought many kilos of candy to distribute to the nurses, doctors, friends, visitors and family as an expression of thankfulness to God. It was also a way of expressing our gratitude to all those who had helped during our trying time.

I could not believe we had a baby all our own. Leah and I were amazed at the little life God had shaped in about forty weeks.

Everything about Gideon fascinated me. His: little fingers, tiny nails, toes, beady eyes, delicate ear, nose, and little lips were all a miracle too wonderful to behold. His little cries, his loud yells, were all new to me.

Since the day Gideon was born, I have forgotten what it means sleep through the night. I do not mean this in a bad way. The first night when Gideon was born, even his loud cry could not wake me up. Leah had to yell out to me so I could wake up, to help her. I was dead to the world. The very next night I became kind of nocturnal. I would awake at the slightest sound Gideon made. Fatherhood had taken over.

Every sound Gideon made was new to our ears. We had to learn to decode these sounds and gurgles. Everyday he did something new. Everyday he seemed to have grown. Gideon took a large part of my time. I could not get my eyes of him. With these surging emotions, also came the swelling load of responsibility. God made me accountable for another life.

Gideon grew so sweetly. He, like most kids, had such an inquisitive mind. He had an endless bank of questions. I tried to answer his questions. To everything I told him, He always asked me "But why, dad?" Memories of Gideon's childhood are so wonderful. He was full of life. He enjoyed everything to the utmost. One thing outstanding, I reminisce about Gideon is his laughter. He laughed from the heart. He is one special child, with a zest for life.

Gideon is 13 years old now. Even as a new teen-ager he lightens every place his presence fills. Another great quality Gideon possesses is his ability to love everything, and everyone. Expressing love is a special gift. Expressing love was difficult, not something I could naturally do. I found it hard to verbalize my love but to Gideon it came naturally. I am getting better at it. I have to constantly make a conscious effort to both verbalize and express love. I have a lot to learn in this area of my life. Gideon brought a lot of joy into our home. He still is a wonderful bundle of joy.

BUBBLY EMERALD

Emy our precious daughter (Emerald) was born on the January 1998. Leah was close to delivery time. We did not know if we were going to have a baby boy or a baby girl. Routine check ups made us drive one hundred and fifty kilometers from Tirupattur in Tamil Nadu state (India) to Bangalore city, Karnataka (India). We had decided to have our second baby in the Church of South India Hospital, where Leah had trained to be a nurse. My parents stayed at Whitefield, Bangalore which is around 15 miles from here.

One morning Leah woke me up saying, "Rich, I am getting pain, let's see if they are consistent." We watched the clock tick, to see if the pains were consistent, just hoping Leah could wait to deliver her baby during hospital hours. Time ticked by, minute-by-minute, hour-by-hour, the pains were consistent. We needed to leave immediately. We had borrowed an old van (belonging to Leah's dad) that would not crank up easily. Finding a group of men, we requested them to help push the van, so we could start her up. Once we got the engine cranked up, we took a 40-minute to an hour drive to the hospital. God got us there safely. Getting there was one big miracle. The doctors examined Leah, coming to a conclusive decision to admit right away. Moments after she was taken to her allotted bed, her pain got intense. Strange, how I felt one with her in all her pain. Since Leah was one of their nurses, they gave her the best care, monitored her progress, allowing her to try to deliver the baby normally. After going through labor pains for about 26 hours, Emerald was born. The nurse brought the good news, "It's a baby girl!" she announced. Leah's family and mine screamed for joy. We could not believe our eyes or ears. Emerald our daughter was born. Both our families had no granddaughters. Emy became the first. Our responsibility doubled. Now we had two children to raise, two kids to answer for.

Emy was different from Gideon. She had big, beautiful, round eyes. She had a shrilly cry. She had a totally different temperament. As Emy grew up, she was much of a 'Tom boy.' Having an older brother, made her play with cars. She was very strong. She could literally break a steel spoon. She had a lot of strength. Gideon loved her. At first, the thought of another baby in the home disturbed Gideon a lot. When Emy finally arrived, Gideon guarded her with his life. On one occasion, the nurse came to get her to take her for a shower. Gideon told the nurse, "Don't touch her, she's mine." Gideon and Emy loved each other dearly. We love them both. Watching them grow has been such a joy. From the moment of their conception, we prayed for their salvation. Today, they are saved. We sincerely pray for God to use them by His grace. Nothing would make us more glad, than to see our children live, work, and walk in ways that please and glorify God. He has entrusted us with a great responsibility to raise them up for Him.

VIBRANT MARCU

Three years down the road after Emy's birth, Marcus was born (2001). He was the tiniest of the three. Marcus was different in every way from his older siblings. He brought home the sounds of a baby we had missed for a while. It was a joy to have him. Unlike Gideon and Emy, Marcus had curly hair, jet black eyes. He had a wonderful smile all his own.

The smell of a baby is quite unique. Gidu and Emy loved caring for Marcus. Marcus grew doing so many funny things, much like a joker. Our bedroom was literally a "bed-room." A queen size bed fit snugly from wall to wall filling one part of the room. Taking advantage of this feature, I built a wooden frame on one side, turning the bed into a big crib. Another single bed fit well, filling the remaining empty space creating an "L." shaped bedding arrangement. This little new arrival, hardly six months old, had a genius of a mind. Though I had tried to form a crib, allowing ample space for his adventures, he felt he was more of an explorer. He tested my carpentry skills, exposing my imperfections at this hobby. Marcus manipulated the frame, opening up the same cross bar to escape his coop each time. Once he had opened up the cross bar, he would crawl out to his free world (onto the other bed). Strangely, each time I fixed the wooded cross bar, he always found a way to open it.

Marcus had his own storehouse of vocabulary. He was full of words. Being the youngest of the family gave him the advantage of picking up words quickly. His sense of humor, funny ways, made him the clown of the family.

Kids watch our every move. Children learn by imitation. I was quite surprised to see how much they observe our actions, emotions, and words. When we first arrived in the US and I started driving, he would tell me when the traffic lights turned red, or green. If he thought I was trying to make it through a traffic light, he'd say, "Dad, you jumped the light." His sense of humor has grown in recent years. He makes all of us laugh. Gidu and Emy too, have a sense of humor all their own. With the arrival of Marcus, our responsibility tripled. Raising children in our present world is not an easy task. Too many dangers lurk around. Prayer is vital. It acts as both the lubricant and the glue. As a lubricant, it helps us have a smooth relationship with God and others. Prayer acts as glue binding the family together. Building an altar in the home is essential. By building an altar I do not mean building a literal altar, but having a place and a prominent time to meet together as a family to pray. Prayer holds us together. It keeps our focus where it ought to be, on God.

Raising three children has got us thinking of the heritage we are going leave behind. We never did have a lot of earthly possessions. We still don't have much. God has taught us to be content. Paul in the New Testament gave his son Timothy this valuable advice (I Tim. 6:6), "But godliness with contentment is great gain." Looking at all God has so graciously given us, we count ourselves greatly blessed. The hymn writer gives a cue to how one can squeeze out an attitude of gratitude. Paraphrasing the sweet words of the hymn, "Count Your Blessings," brings out this message. If you count your blessings one by one, you will be pretty amazed as to how much the Lord has blessed you. When you begin to number them, you will find how numerous they are. Looking back at God's great goodness and faithfulness has changed our future perception of life. Since then, our focus has not been on setting up a material heritage. The Lord drove home this message, riveting it deep down in our hearts. The material desires though always tempting, have gone blurry. The spiritual desires have sharpened and come into focus. God has burdened our hearts to try and lay up a spiritual heritage for our children. Much like the way people store up material wealth for their posterity, a spiritual heritage takes time to build. It must be a conscious effort. Leah and I have given much thought to the spiritual heritage we must leave behind. If we think about laying up this treasure, we can work towards accumulating it. We are working on this savings account. We want to make our spiritual heritage count, so when the time comes we will be able to pass this vast treasure chest down to our children, passing down our family heritage, a legacy all our own.

WHAT KINDS OF HERITAGE ARE WE TO LEAVE BEHIND?

I believe there are at least three types of heritage we are to leave behind. They are: first and foremost, a godly heritage; secondly, an intellectual or mental heritage; and last of all, an emotional heritage.

Earlier we spoke of the divine triangle. Here we speak of the triangular heritage, the kind of heritage we want to leave behind, we must leave behind. Christian homes must leave behind a great spiritual legacy, if we want to be a true reflection of our Great God and Heavenly Father.

A GODLY HERITAGE

If the believer has a right relationship with God, he will have a right relationship with others. If the perpendicular relationship is right, the horizontal one will also be right. God made man with three essential parts: spirit, soul and body. This was the original order. The 'spirit' is that part of man which relates to God. The soul relates to others, and the body relates to self. The fall of man reversed this order. Sin caused man to be selfish. His sin made him think of himself first, others next, and God last. This inverted order can be reversed. Salvation alone can reverse it, so man can make God pre-eminent in his life. Jesus said (John 4: 24), God is a Spirit: and they that worship him must worship him in spirit and in truth." If the spirit is dead, there can be no fellowship. Thus, the unbeliever is unable to commune with a Holy God. The unbeliever's prayer goes unheard. Sinful man is at enmity with the Holy God. God is a Spirit being. Spirit is the highest form of existence. Hence, in order for man to have a restored relationship with God, he must be born of the Spirit. He must be born again. Just as an earthly birth makes him part of an earthly family, spiritual birth makes him part of the family of God, a spiritual family.

Raising our children to know God as their personal savior is the primary responsibility of every parent. Our children need to get saved. Salvation makes it possible for us parents to raise godly children. Salvation resets their priorities. Rebirth makes it possible for any individual to make spiritual decisions. Once a person is born into the family of God, he has the ability to grow as a babe in Christ. Now, it is possible to: guide; teach; help mold that individual. It is possible to help him to stand strong. God has a definite plan for the children we bring forth. He will reveal this to them in time.

Godliness must be the theme of every home. Parents must lead an exemplary lifestyle. A walk with God talks louder than all you can talk about God. Walking with God involves a daily talk with God. It must be very obvious to our children. They ought to find us talking to God. They must see us spending time in prayer (talking to

God). They must see us reading the Bible (God talking to us). Such observations take place when we have personal, daily devotional time alone with God. God enables every member in the family lead a spirit-filled or spirit-controlled life. Personal public prayer (family devotion) is an open display of our dependence upon God. Please be careful to maintain a sincere prayer life. A prayer merely for display produces good hypocrites or actors. Family prayer brings each member of the family to the altar, to God's throne of grace. Meeting at the altar enables it to have a time when needs are openly verbalized. Every member of the family must be given an opportunity to pray for those needs. Once the seed of prayer has been sown, our cares have been turned into prayer. When the seed has been sown and watered, there is nothing much you can do. Though there is nothing exciting taking place on the outward God is working on the inward. All you can do at this time is "Wait" patiently until you see the seed sprout, bloom and blossom. God answers prayer in His perfect time. Seeing His wisdom in answering prayer, strengthen a believer's faith in God. Faith is built up in the home. These are the key aspects of leaving behind a godly heritage. Leaving a godly heritage is pivotal. Leaving behind a rich, strong legacy is vital for the propagation of truth. It is vital for the propagation of the Biblical home. What kind of a legacy are you leaving behind? Are you building a godly heritage so when the time is right, you can give your children a godly inheritance?

AN INTELLECTUAL OR MENTAL HERITAGE

There is a dire need for born again believers to pass down an intellectual heritage. What hinders us to pass down such a heritage? Most religions teach their kids, their religious beliefs at a very young age. They consider it important to pass down their belief system, their heritage. How about Christians? There is a lack of emphasis in teaching the Bible in the modern Christian arena. Are we serious about leaving behind an intellectual heritage? Guess, how much time Muslim kids spend, learning the Koran? An online New York time article, "Memorizing the Way to Heaven, Verse by Verse" has this unbelievable news to deliver, "The children, ages 7 to 14 are full-time students, in class 8 a.m. to 5 p.m., Monday through Friday, even in the summer. But they are not studying math, science or English. Instead, they are memorizing all 6,200 verses in the Koran, a task that usually takes two to three years."[1]

Storing up a rich intellectual heritage requires an investment of quality time. Believers must make it a top priority to study the Word of God. They must accumulate a wealth of Scriptural knowledge, which they can pass down when the time comes. We must not fail to do this. Many drastic changes are taking place in the public schools of America. Derry Brownfield points to one major change in his article *Do your children study the Koran?* "To be politically correct our children are being taught to be tolerant to everybody and everything, regardless of how bizarre it may seem to our American way of life. Public schools are having students learn passages from the Koran and study some of the laws handed down by Mohammed. Our children are taught that Islam is a religion of peace and Allah is just another name for the God of the Holy Bible."[2]

American public schools are beginning to be tolerant to other world religions. Though they forbid prayer in this great Christian country, they permit schools to teach the Koran. Christians must rise to the occasion. Spiritual bankruptcy awaits our next generation if we as parents fail to lay up rich spiritual treasures down to the next generation.

Paul, in II Timothy 1:5 speaks of Timothy's faith which was the result of acquiring an intellectual inheritance. However, let me clarify, salvation cannot be passed down or earned. The Bible makes it clear "For by grace are ye saved through faith; and that not of yourselves: it is the gift of God: Not of works, lest any man should boast." Before Timothy experienced a change of heart, he experienced a change of mind. This mind set was passed down to him. II Timothy 1: 5 tells of the handing down of this intellectual heritage, "When I call to remembrance the unfeigned faith that is in thee, which dwelt first in thy grandmother Lois, and thy mother Eunice; and I am persuaded that in thee also." "Repentance" comes from the Greek word *Metanoeo* meaning, "change of mind." Salvation involves an exercise of faith in the person of the Lord Jesus Christ. It also involves a change of mind. It is the change of the attitude of the mind, from walking against God to walking to and with God. There has to be this change of mind.

I firmly believe the home is the place where all learning begins. The Bible says, Train up a child in the way he should go: and when he is old, he will not depart from it." The Bible is the pillar and ground of all faith. Psalm 119: 89 tells of the surety of God's Word, "For ever, O LORD, thy word is settled in heaven." God's Word stands firm forever. Changing our minds involves changing our attitude towards God. It involves having God in every thought and intent of our minds. Isaiah attests to the stability, strength and security God provides to a person focused on Him. In 26:3-4 he reinstates this thought by saying, "Thou wilt keep him in perfect peace, whose mind is stayed on thee: because he trusteth in thee. Trust ye in the LORD for ever; for in the LORD JEHOVAH is everlasting strength. I have a responsibility to develop my own mind and the mind of my children to honor, serve and please God. This is a Biblical truth. In Romans 7: 25, Paul writes, "I thank God through Jesus Christ our Lord. So then with the mind I myself serve the law of God; but with the flesh the law of sin." Romans 8: 6-7 continues both to dwell and declare the importance of the mind, "For to be carnally minded is death; but to be spiritually minded is life and peace. Because the carnal mind is enmity against God; for it is not subject to the law of God, neither indeed can be." Paul keeps hitting on the same message to drive home the value of having a sound mind. One more reference from Philippians 4: 7 will suffice to chaperon this message. The verse reads, "And the peace of God which passeth all understanding keep your hearts and minds through Christ Jesus." God alone can help us have a sound mind.

The way to have a sound mind is to stay our minds on God. We must fill our minds with thoughts of God and the Word of God. Such a store-house of knowledge can be passed down as an intellectual heritage. Since Philippians 4: 8 sheds great light on this thought, I quote it once more, for the sake of emphasis. It reads, "Finally, brethren, whatsoever things are true, whatsoever things are honest, whatsoever things are just, whatsoever things are pure, whatsoever things are lovely, whatsoever things are of good report; if there be any virtue, and if there be any praise, think on these things." It is important to develop a mental heritage. How can this be accomplished? This can be done by personally storing rich Biblical truths in our minds, then passing them down to our children so they can do the same for their children.

How big is your intellectual bank balance? How much of God's Word do you know? This will be the determining factor as to how much intellectual inheritance you posses and are capable of passing down as a heritage to your children. An intellectual heritage will not save your children. It will make their hearts ready to receive salvation. It will prepare the soil. The word of God is a seed, when planted will bear fruit in due time. This is an assurance we have from the book of Isaiah (55: 11), "So shall my word be that goeth forth out of my mouth: it shall not return unto me void, but it shall accomplish that which I please, and it shall prosper in the thing whereto I sent it."

My greatest concern for my children has been their salvation. From the time Leah and I got married, we prayed that God would in His abundant grace and great mercy, save our children. We did lay a godly, intellectual, Biblical foundation. God prepared their hearts. God graciously saved them. Praise God. Is this something you would like for your children to inherit? You cannot save them but you can prepare them for the time when God will tug on their hearts, then eventually save them. First of all, learn God's Word. Secondly, teach your children the Scriptures. Prepare the soil, their soul. Sow the seed of God's Word in a consistent manner. Plant them in a good Bible believing, Fundamental Baptist Church. These are the vital steps which open up opportunities for God to work in their hearts. Pray for their hearts to be tender and ready to receive God's salvation. God will do His part, but we must do ours. Do all you can, to leave behind an intellectual heritage. It will be worth the investment. I urge you to do so. Once they are saved, they will grow in the knowledge of the Lord Jesus Christ. They will begin to lay up a greater intellectual knowledge base for the next generation.

AN EMOTIONAL HERITAGE

In a world where wrong is right and right is wrong, our children face emotional battles. With the home rapidly crumbling, many children are distraught. I have met such children. They have grown up to be men and women themselves, but they are still as insecure in their hearts as a five to ten year old.

I met a lady in California. She is now in her forties. She told us that her parents had separated when she was a teenager. She is still unmarried. She says, "I am afraid to get married because I might end up like my parents." What an emotionally out of control roller-coaster to be on! She and her sister are unmarried to this day. What terrible results divorce produces!

I met another lady at a Chiropractic College. She was now in her sixties. She told me of an incident which took place in her life. She spoke of a time she would drive on the freeway to get to work. One day, a car behind her lost control and hit her, setting her car on a spin. After having spun many times her car finally came to a halt. This incident caused an emotional scar in her life. She told me, she was never going to use the freeway ever again. It changed her life completely. How do we avoid getting ourselves into an emotional plunge or deluge? How do we untangle ourselves from emotional disasters? Can we avoid them? The answer is yes and no. Yes, we can try not to entangle ourselves from getting into an emotional disaster and no, we cannot escape facing emotional ups and downs if we are part of this world. As human beings we will encounter difficulties, problems and terribly trying emotional situations. But, the truth of the matter is, God can take us through tough emotional times. He can give us the victory. He is well able.

We as adults do not have answers for every emotional problem, but we know the One who does. We know the person that can help, God! We know He can steer us through emotional storms of life. If our children are to survive emotional trauma, we must leave behind a legacy or a rich emotional heritage.

Joy, sorrow, doubt, suffering, anxiety, depression, anger and fear are a few of the numerous emotions every human being encounters in his life. Many grown ups do not know how to handle some of these emotions. Many people come from broken homes. They are raised by a single parent, or have been through a terribly traumatic situation in their life. Some have been through an earthquake, a hurricane or an accident. Some others have faced a drunken dad who yelled or abused their mom both verbally and physically every single day. Such encounters break and shatter many a heart.

When emotions spiral out of control, disaster is about to strike. An emotional tornado is in the making. Just like a mixture of warm and cold air, provide the perfect conditions to give birth to a hurricane, pressures of life create the perfect setting for emotional break downs. Sin has brought man many painful emotions. One such feeling is guilt. Guilt is a terrible emotion to partner with. Men become alcoholics just to overcome guilt. The guilt they feel could be: the feeling they were unwanted as a child, the guilt of doing something wrong emotionally, physically or in matters of finances (such as stealing). Sins such as lying, robbing, molesting, and a multitude of other sins bring a heavy burden of guilt. A man may get away with murder but an overwhelming guilt follows him like a shadow, robbing him of every iota of joy he ever had. Though he may be out there hiding, free for the moment, yet, guilt plagues him every single day. Guilt can result from something very simple such as driving a car with an expired license tag. Conscious wrong doing brings constant fear. The presence of a police car can run shivers through your spine.

We can do better than just survive an emotional rollercoaster. We can be victorious over them. How can we do this? We can! Through God's help and God's help alone, we can be victorious.

THE JOY STEALER

First, let us deal with the deadly emotion of guilt. Satan attacked the very first home attempting to rob the joy they enjoyed. He stole from them their privileges. He tempted Eve to take of the fruit of the tree of good and evil. She did succumb to this temptation. The result, both Adam and Eve experience guilt for the first time in their lives. Guilt overcame them causing them to hide from God. Sin always makes man flee from God's presence. Sin offers man temporary pleasures, but the offer has a heavy price tag. The feeling of guilt is awful. Every man, woman and child born into this world, has to face this emotion. Only Jesus can free you from guilt. When sin is forgiven, guilt can be lifted. Jesus alone can save you from sin, rid you of guilt, and provide rest for your soul. Are you forgiven? Do you carry the load of guilt? Do you desire to be set free? Come to Jesus. Only He can forgive, lift the burden of guilt and set you free.

FREEDOM THROUGH FORGIVENESS

Forgiveness is the greatest gift I have ever received. Through many gospel meetings, God began to tug on my heart. He never did force me to accept Him as my personal Savior. From the time I was little, God began to work on my heart. The more I turned away from God, the burden of sin got heavier. I could bear it no more. One day at last, I decided I had to settle it once and for all. When a preacher preached of how God sent His own Son Jesus into this sinful world, to carry my sin on His own body and die for me on the cruel cross of Calvary, my heart was deeply pricked. Convictions carved deep into my sinful heart. Ashamed of what I put Jesus through for my sin, I sunk under the full load of guilt. Yet, God did not force me to believe on Him. I foolishly fought Him for many years. He kept assuring me, He still loves me. The more I rejected Him, the more He loved me. What an awesome God He is! One night the gospel preacher proclaimed Christ's love for me. He spoke of all the anguish, shame, and ridicule He went through from Gethsemane to Golgotha, Calvary. It was too much to bear. I had watched the movie "Jesus" many times over. That night, God drew me with cords of love unto Himself. I was His prodigal son, lost and wandering, wallowing in sin. He looked out for me, for the day when I would return to Him. Finally, when the message was complete, the altar call was given. I could not hold back. Tears flowed down my cheeks. I knew God was talking to my heart. I repented of my sin. I felt terrible that Christ died for my sin. I was the reason He hung on that cruel cross.

Conviction had finally hit the bull's eye. It had met its mark. Piercing through my hard heart, God had done a perfect work. Fear gripped my being. Looking around me, all I saw was a floor of people. It seemed as though they were watching me. I was afraid to step out. The Holy Spirit nudged me to go up. Finally, staggering, I stood up. Dragging myself up, my feet trembling, I walked up to the altar. I fixed my eyes straight ahead, not looking right or left until I reached the altar. Then, I broke down and cried, "Lord Jesus, please save me, please, please forgive me." I cried out to Jesus, "Lord, if you love me so much, can you please save this wretched sinner?" He did so with open arms. Jesus saved me from sin, cleansed me from all unrighteousness. He took my sins and buried them in the deepest sea. That day, I found freedom, true freedom from sin. Guilt had weighed me down for so long. Finally the weight had been lifted. I was free, free from guilt. I joined the company of those forgiven. I was born again. I was saved. Most of all I became a child of God.

Have you experienced the forgiveness of sin? Has your guilt, been lifted? Trust Jesus as your personal Savior. Romans 10: 9-10 explains how you can be saved, "That is thou shalt confess with thy mouth the Lord Jesus, and shalt believe in thine heart that God hath raised him from the dead, thou shalt be saved. For with the heart man believeth unto righteousness; and with the mouth confession is made unto salvation." Saved at last! What joy flooded my soul! I could say like David, "Blessed is he whose transgression is forgiven whose sin is covered. Blessed is the man unto whom the LORD imputeth not iniquity, and in whose spirit there is no guile." With the forgiveness of sin and the lifting of guilt, comes peace. What is true peace?

PEACE THAT PASSETH ALL UNDERSTANDING

Salvation calms every emotion, bringing it under control. Salvation gives us a peace in the midst of problems. It is because of the one who is in control.

The day I got saved, I surrendered my life to Jesus. I handed over my life's ship. I knew it was the right decision. It is the best decision I ever made. It is wise to trust in an all-wise God. It is best to trust His lead. It is best to follow His all-knowing, omniscient plan. It is best to be sheltered under the wings of His all-powerful, omnipotent hand. He can steer me safely onto heaven's shore.

For a long time in my life, I had been in the driver's seat. It was a mess. All I had done was mess up. I almost wrecked my life many times. Now, I let Jesus pilot my life. I handed it over to His charge. I have peace. I am at peace with God (Romans 5: 1), "Therefore being justified by faith, we have peace with God through our Lord Jesus Christ." We also have a peace that surpasses all. Paul enjoyed this peace while in prison (Philippians 4: 7), "And the peace of God, which passeth all understanding, shall keep your hearts and minds through Christ Jesus." Peace comes when enmity ceases. I was once an enemy of God. I was an alien. Trusting Jesus as my personal savior changed his disposition towards me. Salvation has now made me His child. Therefore, I enjoy God's peace. Do you have this peace? True peace comes when there is real control. I have perfect peace because I know the One in control, is omnipresent, omniscient and omnipotent.

JOY AND SORROW

Jesus is the source of joy. Joy comes because of God, by just being in God's presence (Psalm 16: 11), "Thou wilt shew me the path of life: in thy presence is fullness of joy; at thy right hand there are pleasures for evermore." As human beings, we experience sorrows through many situations such as: sickness, financial loss, death or bad news. David acknowledges sorrow but says (Psalm 30: 5), "For his anger endureth but a moment; in his favour is life: weeping may endure for a night, but joy cometh in the morning." Vine's Expository Dictionary in the PC Study Bible, says this of JOY (NOUN AND VERB), JOYFULNESS, JOYFULLY, JOYOUS:

> Euphrosune 2167 is rendered "joy" in the KJV of Acts 2:28, RV, "gladness," as in 14:17. See GLADNESS.
> Note: "Joy" is associated with life, e.g. 1 Thes. 3:8,9. Experiences of sorrow prepare for, and enlarge, the capacity for "joy," e. g., John 16:20; Rom. 5:3,4; 2 Cor. 7:4; 8:2; Heb. 10:34; Jas. 1:2. Persecution for Christ's sake enhances "joy," e. g., Matt. 5:11, 12; Acts 5:41. Other sources of "joy" are faith, Rom. 15:13; Phil. 1:25; hope, Rom. 5:2 (kauchaomai,

see B, No. 2); 12:12 (chairo, see B, No. 1); the "joy" of others, 12:15, which is distinctive of Christian sympathy. Cf. 1 Thes. 3:9. In the OT and the NT God Himself is the ground and object of the believer's "joy," e. g., Ps. 35:9; 43:4; Isa. 61:10; Luke 1:47; Rom. 5:11; Phil. 3:1; 4:4.[3]

The believer has great hope. Despite all his pain, suffering and sorrow, he can have joy because Nehemiah 8: 10 says, "...The joy of the Lord is your Strength." There could be no better source of joy. God is the believer's source of joy. When you understand that He is in control of every situation, you can have joy in any situation.

THE TERROR THAT STRIKES ALL

Fear is real in our present world. There is the: fear of being robbed; the fear of being kidnapped (loosing our kids), the fear of being murdered, the fear of getting hurt, the fear of getting sick, the fear of death, the fear of earthquakes (living in earthquake country: California). Fear is a good thing to have but it does not need to overwhelm us. While there are genuine things we must fear, there are many things we don't need to fear because we are God's children. Do our infants fear? When something does scare children, they bury themselves in the arms of their parents. Actually, there is a lesson to learn from them. We as adults, try to handle every situation. We pretend to be bold. We don't need to do that, because we can run to God in our time of fear. The Bible exhorts us to not fear.

Abraham was probably afraid that the kings of the east might avenge him because he rescued Lot (Gen. 15). He thought a war might arise out of this situation. The Lord's responds by saying (15: 1), "After these things the word of the LORD came unto Abram in a vision, saying, Fear not, Abram: I am thy shield, and thy exceeding great reward. Abraham is called the Father of Faith, yet he experienced fear.

Isaac, one of the patriarchs was afraid to openly admit that Rebekah was his wife in Gerar, fearing for his own life, thinking the men might kill him for her. When Abimelech discovered the fact that she was his wife, he was afraid. God turned the situation around. Abimelech gave Isaac many privileges. In time, the men of Gerar strove with Isaac's men over a well of water, so he went up to Beer-Sheba. There (Gen. 26: 24), "the LORD appeared unto him the same night, and said, I am the God of Abraham thy father: fear not, for I am with thee, and will bless thee, and multiply they seed for my servant Abraham's sake."

Moses died. Joshua played the role of a servant for many years. He served Moses faithfully. When God took Moses out of the scene, He asked Joshua to lead the Israelites. Joshua was terrified to step into Moses' shoes. The context in the passage in Joshua chapter one, suggests the idea that Joshua was terrified to take on this new role of leadership. God had to encourage him. In verses 5-6a, God says, "There shall not any man be able to stand before thee all the days of thy life: as I was with Moses, so I will be with thee: I will not fail thee, not forsake thee. Be strong and of a good courage." Verse 7a restates, "Only be thou strong and very courageous." Verse nine is the epitome of God assurance, "Have not I commanded thee? Be strong and of a good courage; be not afraid, neither be thou dismayed: for the LORD thy God is with thee withersoever thou goest."

Fearing the Lord is a good thing. Psalm 19: 9a declares, "The fear of the LORD is clean." Proverbs 14: 26-27 speaks of the kind of fear every believer must have, "In the fear of the LORD is strong confidence: and his children shall have a place of refuge. The fear of the LORD is a fountain of life, to depart from the snares of death."

David, the great king of Israel expresses his confidence in God in these words he writes in Psalm (23: 4), "Yea, though I walk through the valley of the shadow of death, I will fear no evil: for thou art with me; thy rod and thy staff they comfort me." The believer needs fear nothing, for the Lord is with him. The shepherd's rod is a symbol of strength. The shepherd tapped his rod assuring the sheep of his presence, when they could not see him around on a foggy night. He used the rod (the hook shaped end) to lift any sheep that fell into a pit or happened to be caught in a thicket. There is the assurance of God's presence and protection. Why must I fear? I need not fear.

Space does not permit us to deal with every emotion. Let me assure you, the Bible has the answers. God who made man can enable us to control our emotions. Knowing God is pivotal. When we have God on our side, emotions can be controlled. Being filled with the Holy Spirit enables us to be controlled by Him. When the Holy Spirit controls us, we have nothing to fear. Many situations may be too big for us to handle as human beings, but to God they are all small.

THE FINALE

Every parent should try to lay up a material inheritance, if possible. The Bible teaches us to do so. Paul writes (II Cor. 12: 14), "Behold, the third time I am ready to come to you; and I will not be burdensome to you: for I seek not yours, but you: for the children ought not to lay up for the parents, but the parents for the children." Some of us may not have too much of a material inheritance but we sure can pass down a Godly inheritance. As parents, we have a great responsibility. To be a parent is one of the most precious gifts anyone can receive. Psalm 127: 3 instructs us that God gives us children, "Lo, children are an heritage of the LORD: and the fruit of the womb is his reward." Proverbs 17: 6 states, "Children's children are the crown of old men." Children are a great blessing. They add joy to the home. However, if they are not nurtured in the ways of the Lord, if they go astray, if they do not receive a rich heritage from us, they will bring much sorrow, in time.

Israel brought heartache and pain to God. Isaiah (1: 2-3) opens up God's heart to reveal His painful cry, "Hear, O heavens and give ear, O earth: for the LORD hath spoken, I have nourished and brought up children, and they have rebelled against me. The ox knoweth his owner, and the ass his master's crib: but Israel doth not know, my people doth not consider." A sad picture indeed! Children are a rich blessing, but with their arrival into our home, there comes a great responsibility that God has laid on our shoulders. The home must be kept from crumbling. There is a way to do it. We can avert this danger, if we parents, pass down a heritage. We must pass down a heritage that is: godly, intellectual, and emotional. Passing down such a rich inheritance will enable our children to succeed, not merely survive here on earth. By ensuring we pass down this heritage, we can help them live victoriously for God. What kind of a heritage are you leaving behind?

CHAPTER EIGHT

THE LITTLE FOXES

Guess you've heard the saying "sly as a fox." The nature of the fox gave rise to this proverb. Foxes are cunning, sly and astute. They are small in stature, but very destructive by nature.

From speaking of the little fox, let us shift our imagination to envision the mighty elephant. Most of us have seen one in a zoo or on television. Most of us probably do not know a lot about elephants. Here is some food for thought concerning these giant creatures, taken from 'Extreme Science':

> Imagine six, full-size pick-up trucks stacked on top of each other. That's how much ***the largest African elephant*** weighed. There are other species of elephants, namely the Asian and the Indian, but they are much smaller than the African. The ***African elephant*** is the king among the giants on land. No other land animal comes close to the size of these creatures. It would take 165 full-grown men to make up the same weight as the world's record African elephant.[1]

Elephants are phenomenal animals. They are extremely large. Did you know the noise of an elephant digesting food can be heard from 600 feet away? Other interesting facts suggest: they drink 15,000 gallons of water; they weigh a lot (the male: 16,500 pounds); they stand 20 feet tall and live approximately 70 years.

Elephants are mighty animals. It would seem they are fearless creatures. Their sheer size makes other animals flee. No animal contemplates fighting them. Though this may be the kind of picture you may draw in your mind, this is not true. The mighty elephants do fear an enemy who is not quite their size. Elephants do fear and flee this deadly, deathly enemy. "Many naturalists and animal hunters in Africa have experienced the strange phenomenon when herds of elephants flee away from ants, known as Army or Legionnaire Ants."[2] No other animal terrorizes an elephant more than this tiny creature. An online article found in "The Deccan Herald" on the "Environment" discloses who these tiny enemies are, that scare these gigantic elephants:

> Forget lions, tigers, and bears! When it comes to the art of attacking, it's Army Ants that will make you break into a cold sweat. Armoured tough, with machete jaws, these masterful fighters hack and dice prey vastly larger than themselves by acting in numbers beyond easy comprehension. Imagine hordes of spear-wielding humans of the Ice Age at a dinosaur's feet. That's the scale of Army Ant operations, when they're attacking any animal, small or big, which crosses their paths. That is why Africa's elephants are not afraid of any animal in their natural environment, except for

Army Ants, which can overwhelm them, if they cannot get out of the path of the marauders.[3]

Lions intimidate every other animal in the jungle. Their sheer size, stature, and stare are sufficient to scare. They have a majestic walk. With every stride "The King of the Jungle" expresses self-confidence. His walk does talk. Big animals do intimidate every other animal. They make all other animals look small. Sometimes, the very look of a Lion, tells the world, "I am boss." Yet, one single animal is not fearful of the Lion's presence. Guess who this animal is? It is the elephant, of course. He even has the audacity to scare this "King of the jungle." Elephants fear none. No animal quite seems to match its size. Yet, this giant fears tiny little creatures, called ants.

Our idea of these tiny ants is about to change. Ants may look small and seem insignificant, but wait till you hear how dangerous and deadly they really are. This story will run a chill down your spine. Why do the elephants fear them? The Deccan Herald continues to unveil this noxious enemy,

> It all starts with a very silent murmur in the area, as millions of Army Ants march in migration in the forests and their billions of feet drum a slow deadly music for all animals (including humans) to get away from their path. A three-lane highway of Army Ants can stretch for as far as 150 yards.
> During its 10-hour workday, an Army Ant colony flows across the forest floor catching thousands of insects and large wounded animals, which cannot run away to escape. Among humans, the individuals who are at highest risk are very elderly people and very young children. The only

saving factor is that the broad front of this army of ants seldom exceeds 20 meters or 65 feet and if you are out of this width, you can be safe and it often takes four hours before these long processions pass any point in its path. In modern days, some African tribes have found out that if you soak the leading columns with kerosene/ petrol and set fire to them, it diverts the main array.[4]

You see why elephants fear them. Though they are tiny, yet they cause panic for the elephant camp. These ants employ a deadly strategy in their attack. Let us learn one final tid-bit of information about these little, destructive creatures,

> These incredibly dangerous insects can grow from 8 mm to 12 mm in length! Most of them are light brown, but some can be reddish. They use formic acid to inject into the bodies of their victims, wrecking the basic circulatory system of all attacked animals.
> It is also considered that Army Ants are some of the most efficient animals, or insects, especially in the tropics. They form a giant group made up of millions of soldier ants. They then march killing and devouring anything in their path. If they come to a large animal, like an entangled cow, the soldiers will gradually start to cover it and when it is totally covered, they will cut the animal into small pieces without touching the internal organs, so it gets eaten alive. After the animal has been cut up into tiny pieces, the worker ants follow a chemical trail to the food and carry it back to the nest. These ants can carry up to 20 times their body weight and rest while consuming their great feast.[5]

Ants not only cause panic amongst the elephant world, they have become a terrible threat to people in Australia. "Recently, the Australian state of Queensland found that it has been invaded by a type of Army Ant, probably brought by cargo ships, and the Queensland Department of Primary Industry says that it'll cost more than $100 million, over the next 5 years, to exterminate these ants." That is a big price to pay to eradicate a tiny enemy. The Army Ant is so deadly, that the Australians are willing to pay a big price to completely eradicate them from their continent. One wonders if they can successfully destroy these "Lilliputs".

The little fox, like the tiny ant, is not to be taken lightly. Never underestimate an enemy. When considering these little enemies, never equate their potential by their mere size. They can wreck havoc. The Bible warns of the danger of ignoring enemies, enemies which threaten our marriages, our homes, our heritages.

Song of Solomon is a romantic book in the Old Testament. It speaks of Solomon's love for the Shulamite woman. It unfolds the enjoyments of love in courtship, also in a marital relationship. Often, this love story symbolizes Christ's love for the church. In this romantic story, in chapter 2: 14, Solomon desires to know everything possible about his fiancée. Verse 15 expresses their desire. Their desire led to a decision. The decision made them determine not to let anything destroy their love for each other. They made a good decision, a wise decision to help secure their commitment. Making a commitment is great. This does not mean everything will be smooth sailing thereafter. The wise King Solomon writes "Take us the foxes, the little foxes, that spoil the vines: for our vines have tender grapes." Marriage is God's design, a venture pioneered by Him. He is its chief architect. Satan in contrast, is a defeated enemy. We are not to underestimate his abilities. He strategically ploys the little foxes belonging to his militia in an endeavor to bring down the strongest homes. He will use every weapon in his artillery to destroy the home. He tries to destroy everything God tries to build. Since, he is a miserable creature; he chooses to make everyone else miserable too.

Foxes are vicious by nature. An online BBC Home article on "Urban Foxes", speaks volumes of their destructive ability.

> A south London couple driven to despair by urban foxes roaming their garden have spent nearly £1,000 trying to keep them out.
> Michael and Susan Sidwell, of Croydon, said they have faced many a sleepless night as foxes fought, howled and screeched in their suburban garden.
> Chicken wire and costly ultra-sonic devices were installed but to no avail.
> The RSPCA said the garden's low fencing, shade and overgrown foliage made it an ideal habitat for foxes.
> Mr. Sidwell said: "I am tired. I have had months of inadequate sleep."[6]

Foxes can wreak havoc in real life. They cause mayhem in marriages. Small things have a way of growing. Soon, they grow so big, they become Goliaths, shouting out threats, instigating fights and arguments. 'Goliaths' are never satisfied; they are relentless, until they totally destroy everything for which we have worked so hard.

The home is a wonderful institution. Guarding it is worth every drop of sweat. It is worthwhile. Great investment of toil and sweat can help build and sustain the home. Hard work will open up opportunities for happiness. Love costs! God, in an expression of love, sent His son Jesus, to die for our wretched sin. He paid a price. Love costs! Love is expensive. In order to keep the fires of love glowing, one must fan it. It requires work. Every marriage requires work. The more you invest, the greater will be your reward. Never ignore the foxes. Be aware of their existence. They creep in unannounced. They pop up in: places you least expect. They come from people you least expect. They creep up from every nook and corner, aiming to destroy what you have built for years. The Internet Center for Wildlife Damage Management has written about the destructive nature of foxes:

> Foxes may cause serious problems for poultry producers. Turkeys raised in large range pens are subject to damage by foxes. Losses may be heavy in small farm flocks of chickens, ducks, and geese. Young pigs, lambs, and small pets are also killed by foxes. Damage can be difficult to detect because the prey is usually carried from the kill site to a den site, or uneaten parts are buried. Foxes usually attack the throat of young livestock, but some kill by inflicting multiple bites to the neck and back.[7]

Little foxes are destructive. This work examines a few little things that ruin a marriage or wreck a home. Little termites can gnaw away wood hidden behind the walls of the house. Someone said, "A stitch in time saves nine". This is a wise quote. It is good advice to follow. We must rise quickly to challenge anything that presents a seeming danger. Guard the home!

LITTLE FOX NUMBER ONE: THE UNTAMABLE BEAST

Little fox number one is an untamable beast, a little member quite capable of inflicting great damage. What could this member be? It is a part of your body. The Bible has this untamable beast in James 3: 2-12,

> For in many things we offend all. If any man offend not in word, the same is a perfect man, and able also to bridle the whole body.
> Behold, we put bits in the horses' mouths, that they may obey us; and we turn about their whole body.
> Behold also the ships, which though they be so great and are driven of fierce winds, yet are they turned about with a very small helm, whithersoever the governor listeth.
> Even so the tongue is a little member, and boasteth great things. Behold, how great a matter a little fire kindleth!
> And the tongue is a fire, a world of iniquity: so is the tongue among our members, that it defileth the whole body, and setteth on fire the course of nature; and it is set on fire of hell.
> For every kind of beasts, and of birds, and of serpents, and of things in the sea, is tamed, and hath been tamed of mankind.
> But the tongue can no man tame; it is an unruly evil, full of deadly poison.

Therewith bless we God, even the Father; and therewith curse we men, which are made after the similitude of God.

Out of the same mouth proceedeth blessing and cursing. My brethren, these things ought not so to be.

Doth a fountain send forth at the same place sweet water and bitter?

Can the fig tree, my brethren, bear olive berries? either a vine, figs? so can no fountain both yield salt water and fresh.

Reflecting on what James mentions here about the tongue will help us evaluate its extremely destructive capability. James uses an entire chapter to discuss this little member. God wants us to bridle our tongues. Much too often, the tongue lands us in so much unwanted trouble. This passage of Scripture teaches the believer both the positive and negative potentials of the tongue. It comparing the tongue to: a bit which controls a powerful horse and a small helm that controls a vast ocean liner. Let us readily glean from the positives. Quickly learn to shun the negatives.

THE POSITIVES

1. The horse can be controlled by a bit
2. The mammoth ships can be controlled by a small helm.
   - ← By way of comparison, we may conclude, it is possible for us to control our tongues. How then can we do this? It can be done only by the help of God. When a believer is filled by the Holy Spirit he can learn to control his tongue.

THE NEGATIVES

If we don't learn to control our little tongues, then the tongue controls us. It causes a world of trouble. Observe the negative effects it produces. This passage declares these facts:

1. The tongue is a fire (set on the fire of hell)
   - It causes a world of iniquity
   - It defiles the whole body
   - It sets on fire the course of nature
   - It is untamable
   - It is unruly
   - Is hypocritical (blesses God and curses men)

Terrible results are produced by the misuse of this little member. James knows of its potential danger. He recognized the great harm it can cause. We ourselves know this to be true. Man has succeeded in accomplishing great feats. To name a few, he has been successful in taming birds, serpents, sea creatures and even the mighty elephant, but has failed miserably in controlling and taming the tongue. Peter gives us a tip to keep our relationships happy (I Peter 3: 10), "For he that will love life, and see good days, let him refrain his tongue from evil, and his lips that they speak no guile." David, the great King of Israel has similar advice (Psalm 34: 12-13), "What man is he that desireth life, and loveth many days, that he may see good? Keep thy tongue from evil, and thy lips from speaking guile." Sound advice indeed!

Arguments often result from the misuse of the tongue. Husbands are provoked to anger by the harsh words of a wife. Wives are hurt and go into depression when husbands fail to use their tongues wisely to express love which edifies them. The wise son of David, Solomon pens these words (Pr 18:21), "Death and life are in the power of the tongue: and they that love it shall eat the fruit thereof." The tongue has the ability to destroy.

By God's grace, we can tame the tongue. God has the ability to transform our tongues, giving it the ability to produce life. David realized the seriousness of the matter when he said (Ps 139:4), "For there is not a word in my tongue, but, lo, O LORD, thou knowest it altogether." Job realized its deadly capability. He prayed (Job 6:24), "Teach me, and I will hold my tongue: and cause me to understand wherein I have erred." He purposed in his heart to use his tongue aright (Job 27:4), "My lips shall not speak wickedness, nor my tongue utter deceit"

James lets us know the tongue is untamable. Yes! It is untamable by us but if we are filled with the Holy Spirit, then it possible for us to use our tongues in a positive manner to produce life. Proverbs 16:1 affirms this very fact, "The preparations of the heart in man, and the answer of the tongue, is from the LORD."

Refrain, is a useful note in music. The ability to refrain from using our tongue is a very simple command. Yet learning to control this little member of our body is so important if we want to be happy people and have happy homes. This is the reason why, the Bible promotes the right use of the tongue. When you are unsure of what to say, just don't say anything at all. Refrain may be used positively. This will help us not unleash our tongues easily. Guarding the tongue from saying whatever we like or expressing our feelings blatantly will keep us from much trouble. Proverbs 21:23 instructs, "Whoso keepeth his mouth and his tongue keepeth his soul from troubles." Harsh use of the tongue builds barriers immensely hard to overcome. In a home the relationship between a husband and wife is tender and harsh words can build barriers in communication. Miscommunication is often a joy and peace stealer. Words often hurt deeply. The effectiveness of a soft answer breaks down barriers in a relationship, proposed in (Pr 25:15), "By long forbearing is a prince persuaded, and a soft tongue breaketh the bone." A soft answer in contrast builds bridges in communication. Another verse of exhortation says (Proverbs 15: 1), "A soft answer turneth away wrath: but grievous words stir up anger."

Lastly, let me point you to one more verse (Proverbs 16:24), "Pleasant words are as an honeycomb, sweet to the soul, and health to the bones." We must determine to use our tongue wisely if we desire to build a home to last a lifetime. A final word of advice on the tongue, take heed, harsh words hurt, but sweet words strengthen and sweeten any bond.

LITTLE FOX NUMBER TWO: THE IMMOVABLE

Laziness kills. As a student in Calvary Baptist Bible College, I heard this statement made by my principal, Dr. Eric Franks, "Hard work never kills." I am not sure who said this but I know this to be true by experience. God has designed the human being for movement. He has given us a body that has hands and feet. These are body parts meant for movement. After God created Adam, He gave him instructions to tend the Garden of Eden. He was designed to work.

Solomon instructs (Proverbs 6: 10) the lazy man to learn a valuable lesson through an object lesson. He turns the sluggard's attention to a tiny creature. The wise king instructs by saying, "Go to the ant, thou sluggard; consider her ways, and be wise." We will discuss some attributes that constitute a lazy man. These attributes help describe his lifestyle. It is hard to find an ant resting. It seems as if they are on an endless mission. God uses them as an object lesson for each man or woman to avoid the sin of laziness. When a man or a woman is lazy, they fail to add structure to the home. Laziness is an undesirable quality, a trait which is self-destructive. Such an attribute fails to support the home.

THE LAZY MAN LOVES TO BE SLOTHFUL

Have you noticed a sloth? It moves ever so slowly. This characteristic earns it its name. It stands as a direct contrast to the little ant. A lazy man is unproductive. A lazy husband provides a poor example, thus he is a weak leader. He cannot lead by example. He fails to command respect. Such men send their wives out to fend for the family. This is very shameful thing for husbands to do. Oft times such men while their time away. Slothfulness is a sin. The Bible says, (Proverbs 12:27), "The slothful man roasteth not that which he took in hunting: but the substance of a diligent man is precious." He is too lazy to roast his game. He had rather let it rot than relish it. He is too lazy to eat. The Bible paints a terrible picture of such a man in Proverbs 19:24, "A slothful man hideth his hand in his bosom, and will not so much as bring it to his mouth again." Lazy men find it hard to eat food that is set before them. Even picking up their food from the plate to their mouth is a surmountable task. When God created man, He designed him for work. God Himself took time to create the earth. He did a work, making man from the dust. He is industrious. He wants us to be industrious and productive. God wants us to be a blessing, not a burden to anyone.

THE LAZY MAN LOVES TO SLUMBER

Rest is necessary. Rest is essential for human beings to recharge, repair and rejuvenate. God is the author who initiated work. He is also the one who mandates rest for man. God exemplified this requirement when He had finished His wondrous creative acts. After He had made man on the sixth day, the Bible says, He rested. In like manner, He wants us to work hard for six days, then, rest on the seventh. Some people never work. All they do is rest, rest and rest. Biblical warnings sound out loud and clear, foretelling the results of too much slumber. In Proverbs 24: 33-34 Solomon writes, "Yet a little sleep, a little slumber, a little folding of the hands to sleep: So shall thy poverty come as one that travelleth; and thy want as an armed man." An idle occupation involving all sleep and no work will eventually bring a man to poverty. His home will be poor. God made Adam responsible to fend for his family, making him the breadwinner (Genesis 3: 19). The woman is designed to be a help-meet. She is to keep the home (Titus 2: 5). Her body is not designed to work like a man. He mind is wired to keep the home. The way she thinks, behaves and views things makes her unique, yet unlike man. God in His infinite wisdom gave each of these individuals their roles. Men and women must take the initiative to fulfill these roles. When they take their respective roles seriously the home functions well. It will be all that God intended for it to be.

THE LAZY MAN LOVES TO STUMBLE

The lazy person always makes excuses. God the great artist paints a good picture of such a person in Proverbs 15:19. It reads, "The way of the slothful man is as a hedge of thorns: but the way of the righteous is made plain." Lazy people find excuses to not do what they ought to do. They greatly exaggerate the situation so as to escape from doing the job that is before them. Proverbs 22:13 reads, "The slothful man saith, there is a lion without, I shall be slain in the streets." He thinks he will die if he ventures out to get a job done. Some lazy men believe work will kill them. But the truth is, work never kills, laziness will. Laziness in such a man is found to be prevalent both in his heart and head. The portrait in Proverbs 21: 25 of this indolent man may be found in the words, "The desire of the slothful killeth him; for his hands refuse to labour." Labor is not easy. Truly a task does require some sweat and tears. However, once you begin to work, it brings satisfaction. How can hard work bring satisfaction? It brings satisfaction because it is what God intended for man.

THE LAZY MAN LOVES TO SQUANDER

Wastefulness is another quality typifying a lazy person. The book of Proverbs contains a wealth of wisdom. In this insightful book the writer discloses another trait of the slothful (18: 9), "He also that is slothful in his work is brother to him that is a great waster." Tragically, the lazy man fails to work. He also squanders all that for which he has not worked hard to earn but has acquired from his father. I have witnessed many such men who while their time away and unashamedly send their wives to work. When she brings home her paycheck, they gamble, drink, smoke, and squander her hard earned money. The Bible calls such a man "a great waster." We must value what we have. We must be good stewards of God's treasures. Every good gift is from God. I must realize my wife is a gift from God. The money He gives me is a gift. I am not to take lightly the things I possess. Time is a gift. We are not to squander it. Life is a gift from God. Every breath we take is borrowed time. Time must be redeemed. Every second lost, is lost forever. Thus, time must never be squandered.

The Scriptures warn a believer not to slothful. The Book of Romans 12:11 warns believers to be, "Not slothful in business; fervent in spirit; serving the Lord." Paul writes urging us in Hebrews 6:12, "That ye be not slothful, but followers of them who through faith and patience inherit the promises." God's children ought to be busy. God gave us an illustration when He created the world. Though God did not need to labor or rest, yet he exemplified both. Jesus worked hard while He was on earth. On one occasion He said (John 9:4), "I must work the works of him that sent me, while it is day: the night cometh, when no man can work." Let us be busy people. Let us be hard working men and women. If we want to succeed building our homes to last a lifetime, we ought to labor for it. Every act to build, demands labor.

LITTLE FOX NUMBER THREE: DISCONTENTMENT

This section addresses those who are not content. The book of Proverbs has a mine of godly advice for those that are willing to dig them up. Digging up Proverbs 15:16 reveals this treasure, "Better is little with the fear of the LORD than great treasure and trouble therewith." Believers ought to learn the art of being content. It is an attitude of the mind. It is attitude we must strive to have on purpose. It is an attitude of gratitude.

Laying up treasures will make us rich. Though they make one rich, they have the aptitude to bring troubles as their companions. Rich people get restless, for they fear the thief. They are uncertain as to who may rob or hurt them. In contrast, the poor man has little, so he rests in peace because has nothing much to lose.

Paul found contentment in his life. In the midst of his perilous life, he found contentment. He shares his secret with young Timothy, his son in the faith (Phil 4:11), "Not that I speak in respect of want: for I have learned, in whatsoever state I am, therewith to be content." In Timothy, he has this valuable advice for his beloved son in the Lord (1 Tim 6:8), "And having food and raiment let us be therewith content." The author of Hebrews (13:5) exhorts us to live contented lives, "Let your conversation be without covetousness; and be content with such things as ye have: for he hath said, I will never leave thee, nor forsake thee." This is an assurance of God's presence. God's presence assures us of His provision. Hence, there is no need to fear. Contentment is a state wherein the believer makes a willful choice of not trusting in self, but trusting God to provide for his needs. In the wilderness, some of the Israelites were afraid to take God at His word. God had told them to gather sufficient manna for each day's requirement. Some distrusting Jews gathered more. Exodus 16:18 explains the result of failing to be content or trust God. It reads, "And when they did mete it with an omer, he that gathered much had nothing over, and he that gathered little had no lack; they gathered every man according to his eating."

Contentment brings joy. Joy results in satisfaction. Contentment is not limited to money or things. Its boundaries reach far beyond. Its tentacles reach into relationships as well. In the realm of relationships, contentment means the husband must be thankful for his own wife. The wife ought to be content with her own husband. God made one Eve for Adam, not many EVES. When we cherish what God has given us, we can find contentment.

Unthankfulness stems from the roots of discontentment. Unthankfulness leads down a path causing us to commit terrible, unimaginable sins. The steps of an unthankful heart are always downward. Romans 1: 21-22 reads, "Because that, when they knew God, they glorified him not as God, neither were thankful; but became vain in their imaginations, and their foolish heart was darkened. Professing themselves to be wise, they became fools." How unwise it is to be unthankful. Notice further, the deadly results produced by unthankful heart. Paul continues to describe its deadly descent in Romans 1: 23, "And changed the glory of the uncorruptible God into an image made like to corruptible man, and to birds, and fourfooted beasts and creeping things." Let us learn the art of contentment. It will result in us having a heart of contentment.

LITTLE FOX NUMBER FOUR: PRIDE

Pride is creepy. It is a very deceptive sin. Every human being possesses some measure of pride. Pride is never a good trait.

Discovering I was a sinner, I realized, there was nothing good in me. There was nothing I could boast about. I learned I was totally depraved. I deserved to go to hell. There is no good in me, means, I was wretched, undeserving, the worst of all sinners. I understood, as a sinner, I deserve nothing good. All I ever deserve is God's judgment. When God could easily mete out judgment, He extended His goodness to me. God saved me. Salvation brought manifold blessings. God blessed me with so many spiritual blessings. I realize I am truly blessed. I realize now, the greatest miracle of all God had performed was saving me, a wretched sinner, solely by His Grace.

PRIDE HAS ITS ORIGIN

I John 2:16 classifies sin into three categories by stating, "For all that is in the world, the lust of the flesh, and the lust of the eyes, and the pride of life, is not of the Father, but is of the world."

Pride always goes before a fall. Satan, the father of this world was filled with pride. It was the one deadly trait which brought him down, creating the scenario for his downfall. Pride cost Satan a lot. It cost his God-given position. He was the highest of all God's created beings. He lost this wonderful privilege, merely because he allowed the sin of pride to control him (Ezekiel 28; Isaiah 14). Pride originated with Satan. Anything originating from him can never be good or beneficial to man. Jesus on the other hand was humble. He has so much to be proud of, but He humbled Himself. He knows the danger pride poses. God hates this awful sin. He wants His children to take heed of this deadly sin.

PRIDE IS DANGEROUS

GOD HATES PRIDE

Solomon states (Proverbs 6:16-17), "These six things doth the LORD hate: yea, seven are an abomination unto him: A proud look, a lying tongue, and hands that shed innocent blood." God hates pride. When one partner in a marriage bond is proud, there is bound to be trouble. Pride hurts the home. It is a sin that ebbs from a selfish heart. Pride seeks to satisfy self. It craves to gratify self. It seeks pleasure even though the pleasure it seeks may only come by way of causing pain to the other partner.

Pride creates a wall, a hurdle. It hinders us from admitting our wrong. No wonder it is a sin God hates. It is the very reason it tops Solomon lists in the Scripture passage quoted above. Here are some reasons why God hates this terrible sin. The reasons are as follows:

God hates pride, so He resists the proud

James says (James 4:6), "But he giveth more grace. Wherefore he saith, God resisteth the proud, but giveth grace unto the humble."

God hates pride because it brings contention

Proverbs 13: 10 discloses its destructive capability, "Only by pride cometh contention: but with the well advised is wisdom."

God hates pride because it always results in a fall

Proverbs 16:18-19 states, "Pride goeth before destruction, and an haughty spirit before a fall."

God hates it because it is destructive

He admonishes us to take heed by changing our attitude. Verse 19 admonishes the believer to have a humble attitude, "Better it is to be of an humble spirit with the lowly, than to divide the spoil with the proud."

God hates pride because of the downfall in brings

Pride has the ability to bring us down, one way or another. Nebuchadnezzar could well attest to this truth because he experienced its painful sting firsthand. While boasting of his accomplishments, he said to himself, "Is not this the great

Babylon that I have built....?" This was clearly a statement which angered God. His rebellious attitude was evidenced by his prideful spirit. As a result, the story records God's judgment upon this proud king. The king learned how foolish it is for a man to engage himself in the sin of pride. He understood the futility of having a boastful spirit. Daniel records Nebuchadnezzar's confession (Dan 4:37), "Now I Nebuchadnezzar praise and extol and honour the King of heaven, all whose works are truth, and his ways judgment: and those that walk in pride he is able to abase."

Paul the great apostle, a rebel at first, fought a losing battle against the early church. In his zeal, he cast believers in prison, causing havoc in the church. Later, after his salvation he set aside his pride. Paul understood the grace of God very well. This lesson had burned its way deep into his soul. Now, he realized he did not deserve anything from God. His humble spirit caused him to pen Galatians 6:14, "But God forbid that I should glory, save in the cross of our Lord Jesus Christ, by whom the world is crucified unto me, and I unto the world."

Pride is a battle you may win and yet lose. It destroys, deceives and demolishes everything we want to build. Let's not give any room for pride in our homes. Pride will bring contention. Contention always is hurtful. The results are always destructive. It could well be the very agent of destruction Satan may use to make your home crumble.

LITTLE FOX NUMBER FIVE: JEALOUSY

Solomon tells of this little fox's destructive ability in Song of Solomon 8:6, "Set me as a seal upon thine heart, as a seal upon thine arm: for love is strong as death; jealousy is cruel as the grave: the coals thereof are coals of fire, which hath a most vehement flame." The book of Proverbs provides more information about this little fox named jealousy in (6:34-35), "For jealousy is the rage of a man: therefore he will not spare in the day of vengeance. He will not regard any ransom; neither will he rest content, though thou givest many gifts."

When this little fox 'jealousy' creeps into our homes, he brings untold misery and heartache. Jealousy is never satiable until it sees the total destruction of other partner. Thus, Solomon says it is "cruel as the grave." When a person is filled with jealousy, nothing can appease or pacify. The following verses reveal the true colors and conditions of jealousy:

> A sound heart is the life of the flesh: but envy the rottenness of the bones." (Proverbs 14: 30)
> For we ourselves also were sometimes foolish, disobedient, deceived, serving divers lusts and pleasures, living in malice and envy, hateful, and hating one another. (Titus 3:3)

> Being filled with all unrighteousness, fornication, wickedness, covetousness, maliciousness; full of envy, murder, debate, deceit, malignity; whisperers. (Romans 1: 29)
>
> Wrath is cruel, and anger is outrageous; but who is able to stand before envy? (Proverbs 27:4)

Jealousy always boils out of an unthankful heart. It is a natural trait often found in unbelievers. Believers ought to be different. Once saved, the believer's love should cause him to rejoice over his brother rather than envy him.

Jealousy as a sin is a very grave one because it has the capacity to easily creep into a marriage. Strange as it may seem, we could be jealous of our spouses. This is a sad truth. This sin can break up a home. The marital relationship is a joint venture. It is not a tug-of-war. It must be like the many engines of a huge freight train. Those engines work together, pulling its cargo. Partners in marriage rise and fall together. The success of one is the success of the other. The victory of one partner should never cause the other to breed jealousy, rather it should bring joy.

How can one overcome jealousy? Can it be overcome? The answer is a positive one, "Yes." Jealousy may be overcome with love. Love can enable us to celebrate the success of our spouse. Love can rejoice in the blessing others receive. Love does not envy. Love is never jealous.

God's Holy Spirit that dwells within us can help us overcome jealousy. We cannot fight this deadly enemy on our own. It will creep up on us, even take us by surprise. Its tentacles slowly edge their way into our lives, until they get a deathly grip upon us. It will crush the one we love.

One final warning, remember, jealousy has a very cruel side to it. It is cruel as the grave. It is only satisfied when it sees the other person in the grave. If we are not careful, it will see the end of the one we pledged to live with, causing us to break our commitment to "till death us do part." Let us beware of this little fox.

LITTLE FOX NUMBER SIX: UNFAITHFULNSS AND SELFISHNESS

When we are not content with the wife, the home, the things God has given us, we lust after other things. Joy comes when we enjoy our God given gifts. Back in the Garden of Eden, sorrow came as a result of desiring the forbidden fruit. If Adam and Eve were content with all the wonderful fruits God had graciously allowed them to enjoy, they would have stayed out of harm's way. Their desired the one forbidden fruit. This desire landed them in deep trouble. God sets boundaries to protect us. He warned Adam and Eve of the danger of disobedience. Genesis 2: 17 records God's warning, "But of the tree of the knowledge of good and evil, thou shalt not eat of it: for in the day that thou eatest thereof thou shalt surely die." Sin brings death. Sin separates. Sin steals our joy. The sin of unfaithfulness and selfishness shifts the focus from God to me.

Selfishness and unfaithfulness go hand in hand. When our thoughts are all self-centered we think like the Devil. Our thoughts are often only of ourselves, and nothing of others. With such a mindset we tread precariously into enemy territory.

God made Eve to fill the void in Adam's life. God wanted Adam to care for his wife, provide for her and protect her. Like Adam we are to think of our wives. We are to care for them. We are to treasure them. Selfishness will defeat God's plan for marriage. It must be defeated. It is a deadly enemy. Solomon, the wisest man in the world failed to stay faithful. He warns of the danger of seeking selfish, sinful pleasures. He cautions us to beware of the women out in the world who choose to destroy and lure us into lusting after them. Unfaithfulness will ruin our homes. Solomon, from personal experience asks us to be vigilant (Proverbs 7:21-23) because the lustful woman prowls about looking for a victim. He warns, "With her much fair speech she caused him to yield, with the flattering of her lips she forced him. He goeth after her straightway, as an ox goeth to the slaughter, or as a fool to the correction of the stocks. Till a dart strike through his liver; as a bird hasteth to the snare, and knoweth not that is it for his life." Preserving the home demands each partner's willingness to make definite sacrifices.

Solomon begs God's people to take heed. His failure brought awful results. Painful memories filled his mind because he failed to heed God's Word. Wisdom does not guarantee a right or righteous walk with God. Wisdom in and of itself did not safeguard the wisest man in the world. He did not escape from the sin of sexual impurity. Wisdom fails to protect from this vicious sin. Obedience to God's Word alone is our only hope. Volumes of books on wisdom cannot protect us, but wisdom turns into values when we simply follow through with the message of a small, two-letter word "DO." This is a Bible word. The synonyms for the word "DO" are "Keep," and "obey." Heed the wise king's plea (Proverbs 7: 25-27), "Let not thine heart decline to her ways, go not astray in her paths. For she hath cast down many wounded: yea, many strong men have been slain by her. Her house is the way to hell, going down to the chambers of death."

Keep in mind, God is the architect of the home. He knows what is best for you. He has given you the right helpmeet. He wants your homes to be strong, sturdy, and sure. When the home crumbles, the husband is the one responsible. He is the one to be blamed. God does not want me or my marriage to fail. He is ever willing to help me steer my family on the road to marital success if only I am humble enough to ask. Let us request, beg, and plead, the help of the wisest Architect of marriage. Don't we want to succeed in building our homes?

LITTLE FOX NUMBER SEVEN: DOUBT

Satan planted the first seed of doubt. Doubt is a terrible sin. The first two sins found way back in the book of Genesis are selfishness and unbelief. These sins caused Adam and Eve to doubt the God who created them. God created Adam and Eve with no blemishes. They were perfect in every way. However, He did not make a computerized human to be a robot. A robot does not have the capacity to foster a relationship. Thus, God made man with a free will. Man was at liberty to use his free will to make choices. God gave him ample freedom, only restricting him from eating the fruit of one tree.

Satan approached Eve, speaking deceitfully to her. Genesis 3: 1 unfolds the drama of that fateful day, "Now the serpent was more subtil than any beast of the field which the LORD God had made. And he said unto the woman, Yea, hath God said, Ye shall not eat of every tree of the garden?" He planted the seed of doubt. The drama soon reveals the dilemma facing Eve. Anytime a seed is planted, it will sprout if the conditions are right. Eve failed to shun the doubt Satan planted. She failed because she was not near the presence of God. Every sin is a direct result of being distanced from God. Rather than responding to God in simple obedience, she responded to Satan's temptation and believed his lie. All sin is a direct result of distrusting truth. Doubt is caused because of a little lack in the exercise of complete trust. Communicating with the enemy could lead to compromise. Eve learned this lesson. The slightest compromise jeopardizes the attainment of true spirituality.

Next, communicating with the enemy led to contemplating his lie. Pondering the thought (seed) he had planted, led to performing the perilous sin. God in love had graciously forewarned of this peril.

Love always looks out for the one loved. Finally, in her selfishness and unbelief, she succumbed to Satan's wily trap (Gen. 3:6). "And when the woman saw that the tree was good for food, and that it was pleasant to the eyes, and a tree to be desired to make one wise, she took of the fruit thereof, and did eat, and gave also unto her husband with her; and he did eat."

Sin always carries a painful price. The Bible tells us sin is costly. Sin cost man "death." Sin cost God His Son. The Bible declares death to be the wages/payment for sin. Death for the unbeliever is terrible because it is an eternal separation from God. The Bible states in Romans 6:23 that "the wages of sin is death." Adam and Eve were at liberty to exercise their free will. They were completely free to freely exercise their free will. They could have chosen to do right. They willfully chose not to trust God's truth. Choosing to believe the Devil caused them to doubt the true God. It brought upon them a terrible penalty, eternal death. Notice how serious a sin this was. No sin is small in God's eyes. Sin is sin. This was an eternal sin. Because eternal God created an eternal being, the sin he commits is eternal in nature. Only an eternal God can forgive eternal sin. He alone can provide eternal salvation. God in grace and mercy extends eternal salvation to those who call upon Him.

Satan has been successful in destroying homes. He uses the weapon of doubt to do so. We must not stop this howling Goliath. How do we overcome his threat? The answer is plain and simple.

Stop doubting God. Stop doubting His Word. The opposite of doubt is 'trust.' We must first learn to trust God. Don't ever doubt His Word.

God is trustworthy. God's immutability makes him trustworthy. He never changes. His Word never does change. We must build a wall of trust in our families. Since man is created in the image of God, we can reflect trust. We are fallible. However, with God's help we can learn to build in us the trait of trust.

Husbands need to provide a feeling of security by building trust in their wives and vice versa. Neither partner should give occasion, for the other to doubt his/her loyalty. As we have examined, doubt always arises when there is a lack of trust. Communication fosters trust, eliminating all possible doubt. Other doubt-causers could be: suspicious behavior; lack of transparency; unaccountability of personal time, finances, or secretive external relationships.

Loyalty or faithfulness is a rare jewel. It is a rare find. Proverbs talks of this priced treasure in (20: 6), "Most men will proclaim every one his own goodness: but a faithful man who can find?" Faithfulness is a rare character commodity. The little fox of doubt may tiptoe into our homes. Husbands and wives must maintain a pure, holy, loyal relationship with God and with each other. Such qualities produce trust. Let us not let the little fox of doubt destroy our homes.

A QUICK FLASH BACK

After I got married, I had to battle some serious situations in order to preserve my marriage. God taught me many valuable lessons during this early phase of my married life. I was brought up in a home of three boys. Living with my wife (a woman) brought new challenges. I had to learn to share everything with her. This was not easy. I had to consciously choose to care for her before I thought of myself. Issues of selfishness confronted me. When they did, rather than confessing and putting them behind me, I argued. In trying to justify myself, I blamed others for the wrongs I had done. God never let me scheme my way out of these situations. He wanted me to learn to overcome and defeat these enemies in my life. In time, I have learned to be more unselfish. Selfishness comes naturally. I don't need to work at it. Unselfishness, sharing, and giving go against my nature. I have to constantly seek God's help through prayer and keep on working at it. God sent me through many trials. These trials have tested my metal. Fire always tries. Trials bring discomfort. They bring to light many hidden traits and unpleasant feelings. It is never easy to go through a trial. However, there is a bright side to trials, they purify us.

Marriage is not a bed of roses. For every rose in a stem, there are many thorns. Many threats confront a home, a marriage. Nobody needs be overwhelmed by them. Focus on destroying one threat at a time. Truthfulness, honesty, transparency, loyalty, faithfulness, purity, and a holy lifestyle nurture trust. Remember, someone said, "Trust begets trust." No home is trouble proof, worry proof or doubt proof. Every home will be exposed to vehement dangers. When either spouse is at fault for causing the home to quiver, he/she must seek to reconcile quickly. The Bible says (Eph, 4:26), "Be ye angry, and sin not: let not the sun go down upon your wrath." Quick reconciliation brings quick remedy and restoration. Forgiveness is a wonderful gift God has extended to every believer. We must be quick to forgive and quick to forget. Satan waits to breed bitterness. He uses bitterness as a wedge to split the home. Those who are wise heed God's advice, guarding against the wiles of the Devil. I must admit I have failed many times. God is teaching me to acknowledge my failures. Learning to forgive and seek forgiveness quickly has helped my home get stronger.

God is still working on me. I am learning to follow God's lead. I had to defeat many little foxes in my life, the little foxes called: selfishness; pride; anger; envy and jealousy, just to name a few. Little foxes still pop up now and again.

At first, I tried to defend myself. It came naturally for me to quickly point a finger at someone else. Now, I try to pray like David (Ps 139:23, 24), "Search me, O God, and know my heart: try me, and know my thoughts: And see if there be any wicked way in me, and lead me in the way everlasting." Walking in the fear of the Lord enables me to walk in wisdom. We need God's help, God's wisdom, and God's power to overcome the little foxes that tirelessly try to rummage and wreck our home. I must be ready to stand up to any threat coming my way. I must destroy them with God's help, or they will destroy my marriage and my home. Victory is ours to claim. The Bible says (Romans 8:37), "Nay, in all these things we are more than conquerors through him that loved us." We can defeat the little foxes. We surely can defeat every one of them. With God's help, we can. Yes, we can!

CHAPTER NINE

EXCEPT THE LORD BUILD THE HOME

"Except the LORD build the house, they labour in vain that build it: except the LORD keep the city, the watchman waketh but in vain." This verse is found in the book of Psalm 127: 1. The Lord is not involved in building a house. He is surely excited about building a home. We ought to be excited about it too. As we have discussed, in a world of lopsided values, people spend more time and energy building a house, rather than a home. The LORD alone can help build the home.

THE MEANING OF THE WORD "BANAH"

Building anything useful is a constructive endeavor. The word *BANAH* means to build. God has given us the verse in Psalm 127: 1 to clearly establish the need to involve God in all our plans, projects and purposes. *The Adam Clarke Commentary* explains the verse well,

1. To build the temple of the Lord, which was called habayit (heb 1004), the house, by way of eminence.
2. To build any ordinary house, or place of dwelling.
3. To have numerous offspring.

In this sense it is supposed to be spoken concerning the Egyptian midwives; that because they feared the Lord, therefore he built them houses. See the note at Exo. 1:21. But, however, the above passage may be interpreted, it is a fact that been (heb 1121), a son, and bat (heb 1323), a daughter, and bayit (heb 1004), a house, come from the same root baanah (heb 1129), to build; because sons and daughters build up a household, or constitute a family, as much and as really as stones and timber constitute a building. Now it is true that unless the good hand of God be upon us we cannot prosperously build a place of worship for his name. Unless we have his blessing, a dwelling-house cannot be comfortably erected. And if his blessing be not on our children, the house (the family) may be built up, but instead of its being the house of God, it will be the synagogue of Satan. All marriages that are not under God's blessing will be a private and public curse. This we see every day.[1]

A great responsibility has been entrusted to us by God. He has given us the responsibility to build the home. Just as Noah built the ark, Moses built the tabernacle, and Solomon built the temple by God's dictates, so also, we ought to build the home by His dictates. God gave specific instructions to Noah, Moses and Solomon. Noah built an ark. Even though it faced the great deluge, it did not sink. He ventured to build the ark with absolutely no prior experience in shipbuilding. In a worldly context, he was unqualified for the job. Moses built the tabernacle. This place of worship could easily be pitched or relocated at any given time. It was a structure they could erect or take down quickly. God's wise design of the tabernacle made it possible to easily transport and transplant it in anywhere in the burning desert. Solomon fulfilled David's desire for building the temple. David could not settle down in his palace while there was no earthly structure to house God. Solomon fulfilled his father David's desire to build God a house. He built the temple by following the instructions God gave him. God's manual for building the ark did not require any rationalization or renovation on Noah's part. Though God's directions seemed unreasonable, Noah unquestioningly obeyed. The plan and proposition is recorded in Genesis 6: 14-16.

> Make thee an ark of gopher wood; rooms shalt thou make in the ark, and shalt pitch it within and without with pitch. {rooms: Heb. nests}
> And this is the fashion which thou shalt make it of: The length of the ark shall be three hundred cubits, the breadth of it fifty cubits, and the height of it thirty cubits.
> A window shalt thou make to the ark, and in a cubit shalt thou finish it above; and the door of the ark shalt thou set in the side thereof; with lower, second, and third stories shalt thou make it.

Noah expressed trust in God just through simple obedience. He had no prior model to follow. He had not seen any other ark before. He had nothing to compare it with. He could make no comparison. Nothing like the ark had ever been built. He could not evaluate the ark's design and dimensions based on any other building or monument. He had to trust God completely. Another fact was he had never seen rain, let alone an ark. Obeying an all-wise God is an all-wise choice.

Moses was well educated. He was brought up in the palace of Pharaoh. He was used to being in-charge. He was well accustomed to giving orders. Roles reversed when God ordered him to build the tabernacle. Now, it was his turn to take orders. He was humble enough to accept them. Obeying God's orders may have often gone against his human reasoning. His earthly knowledge contradicted divine design and direction, yet he trusted God. Man's wisdom is finite, God's, infinite. It is not worth comparing.

God instructs Moses to build the tabernacle. His instructions are found in Exodus 25:9, "According to all that I shew thee, after the pattern of the tabernacle, and the pattern of all the instruments thereof, even so shall ye make it." Dr. Roy Wallace, in his book, "Lessons from the Tabernacle" mentions, "In Exodus 25 God met with Moses on Mount Sinai and described to him exactly how the Tabernacle should be built. Every detail was designed by Almighty God and every part had a typical, prophetic, or redemptive significance. God, Himself was the architect and He designed it in such a way that every detail pointed to some aspect of the character and work or the person of His son, the Lord Jesus Christ."[2]

God always does things with greater insight. God's omniscience enables Him to have a wholesome, knowledgeable, intelligent view of everything. Man has a horizontal view. God's view envisions everything from a bird's eye view. Notice how Moses responds to God's command. "And Moses did as the LORD commanded him; and the assembly was gathered together unto the door of the tabernacle of the congregation." This verse (Leviticus 8: 4) exposes Moses' obedient heart. He did exactly what the Lord commanded him, from start to the finish. The Bible records God's desire with these two words "Thou shalt," stressing the fact; God wanted the Tabernacle to be built His way, and no other way.

David dwelt in an incredibly beautiful palace. He did not feel comfortable to live there because God dwelt amongst the curtains. This was a good desire. However, God cannot be contained in a building or a picture. Since God is omnipresent, God cannot be limited by space or time. God's answer to David's desire came through Nathan the prophet, "Go and tell my servant David, Thus saith the LORD, Shalt thou build me an house for me to dwell in? Whereas I have not dwelt in any house since the time that I brought up the children of Israel out of Egypt, even to this day, but have walked in a tent and in a tabernacle." God did not permit David to build Him a house, for David's hands were full of blood from the battles he had fought. God did consent to his preparing the things required for setting up a house for Him, but stated that Solomon would build it (I Chronicles 22: 10). Solomon did end up building the Temple under God's divine direction.

Each of these men succeeded in completing what seemed to be an insurmountable task. This is a valuable lesson for every believer who wishes to build a home and succeed at it. *Vine's Expository Dictionary of Biblical Words* tells us the word "BUILD" in the Bible (also used in Psalm 127: 1) comes from the Hebrew word,

> Banah 1129, "to build, establish, construct, rebuild." This root appears in all the Semitic languages except Ethiopic and in all periods of Hebrew. In biblical Hebrew, it occurs about 375 times and in biblical Aramaic 23 times.
> In its basic meaning, banah appears in Gen. 8:20, where Noah is said to have "constructed" an ark. In Gen. 4:17, banah means not only that Enoch built a city, but that he "founded" or "established" it. This verb can also mean, "to manufacture," as in Ezek. 27:5: "They have made all thy ship boards of fir trees...." Somewhat in the same sense, we read that God "made" or "fashioned" Eve out of Adam's rib Gen. 2:22."[3]

God used the word *Banah* on purpose. He wants every home to depend entirely on Him. He alone provides the home with the strength and stability it requires to stand strong. This word: "Banah can also refer to "rebuilding" something that is destroyed. Joshua cursed anyone who would rise up and rebuild Jericho, the city that God had utterly destroyed Josh. 6:26."[4]

Psalm 127: 1 first establishes the believer's need to have God as the chief architect to aid in building his home. This verse stresses the fact that God is the "Producer" of the home. Verse two emphasizes He is the "Protector" of it. The rich people of this world are able to buy a house, a bed, but cannot find rest in either. It regards to this the wise Psalmist notates, "It is vain for you to rise up early, to sit up late, to eat the bread of sorrows: for so he giveth his beloved sleep." The believer need not worry about a thing. He need not be restless, for He has God to protect him. He has a God who can give his eyelids sleep. During Nehemiah's rebuilding of the Jerusalem wall, the work was in progress around the clock. People who labored (built 'the wall' and protected 'themselves') during the day, rested at night, while those who labored at night, rested during the day.

THE METAPHORICAL MEANING OF THE WORD "BANAH"

The word *Banah* has a metaphorical or figurative use. *Adam Clarke's Commentary* explains this shade of meaning:

> Metaphorically or figuratively, the verb banah is used to mean "building one's house"— i. e., having children. Sarai said to Abram, "I pray thee, go in unto my maid; it may be that I may obtain children by her" Gen. 16:2. It was the duty of the nearest male relative to conceive a child with the wife of a man who had died childless Deut. 25:9; he thus helped "to build up the house" of his deceased relative. Used figuratively, "to build a house" may also mean "to found a dynasty" 2 Sam. 7:27.[5]

The meaning indicates the vitality of involving God in the founding of the family, the erecting of the home. I do like the way it can be used figuratively "to found a dynasty." It accentuates the importance of the heritage. In the book "Your Heritage" written by J. Otis Led Better and Kurt Bruner the subtitle reads "How to be intentional about the legacy you leave." Yes, with God's help we must found: a dynasty of faith; a spiritual dynasty; an intellectual dynasty; an emotional dynasty and a godly dynasty, for the Lord. This is our only hope, our ultimate lifeline. We have to be intentional about leaving behind a rich, vibrant, spiritual and godly heritage.

Psalm 127 got interwoven in my early Christian life of faith. It penetrated deep within my very bones, sinews and marrow. It became part and parcel of everything I did. I purposed before I got married or even started a home, to inculcate God in the founding and establishing of my home. Leah and I willfully made this decision. Every husband and wife must make a conscientious choice. You may ask "Is your home perfect? I honestly would reply with an affirmative, "NO!" In fact, it is far from perfect. We are still building and renovating as God's dictates. Yet, I am absolutely certain I am trying to on purpose, build with a great determination, a Biblical, Baptistic legacy. I want to leave for my children, and all future generations such a heritage. With God's help, my wife and I can succeed building a home that glorifies God. This is my one desire. It is my most fervent prayer. "For of him, and through him, and to him, are all things: to whom be glory for ever. Amen." If we have God as our source, supply and strength, we can make this happen. He desires we glorify Him by simply following through with His plan. This is God's design and purpose for every home (Romans 11: 36).

THE BUILDING BLOCKS

The building blocks of marriage must have these ingredients, primarily God, secondarily the husband and the wife. To this structure God adds, children. For the home to be established well, the Bible provides strong guidelines. Since, the home is God's idea, it is wise to spend time studying God's Word to understand His guidelines. While doing my doctoral dissertation, I purchased a book entitled; *I'll Meet You at the Northeast Corner of Heaven*. The title of the book made me curious so I wanted to find out why the author gave it such a title. I'd like to share with you, how Barbara Butler Norrell the author, chose her title. Here's how, in her own words:

> Soon after the terrorist tragedy of September 11, 2001 (i.e., the bombing of the World Trade Center in New York City), my husband Larry walked into the kitchen as I was preparing breakfast for our son. He said, "You know, Barb, if this world should end today, I'll meet you and Luke at the northeast corner of heaven." My first response was, "What?" after he repeated himself, I asked, "Could you be more specific?" Then Larry said, "Well how specific is that? It's a one-foot space at the corner. I'll meet you there, Okay?" I agreed, and he walked out the door on his way to work.[6]

How wonderful "I thought." How can we be assured, we will meet each other on the Northeast Corner of Heaven? Love is the key.

Why The Home Crumbles

Love has to be one other key ingredient in such a structure. Marriage is a bond made for a lifetime. When God planned the home, he designed it to comprise of permanent relationship. No human being should ever try to break up a home because God established it to last for life. If this is God's design, I want my home to last forever. I want my kids to build such homes. We cannot imagine the joy it would bring to our hearts. The Bible has in its pages the blue print reveling the Chief Architect's mind. It is up to you and me to use its precepts. You may choose to follow its directions, to establish a firm foundation. Use it to erect the pillars. Use it to establish the structure. Use it to finish the building. Use it to build an extremely durable home.

The church at Corinth had many problems. Being a city located on the seaport was one reason it brought in many unhealthy waves of trends. Seaport cities are known for their wickedness. Many sinful practices influenced the church. Paul instructed the young Corinthian church, teaching them how to act and react to the problems confronting them. Homes were dangerously poised, tossed by the turbulent trends of the huge seaport city. These dangers caused Paul to address some major issues on "marriage." Paul's letter to the Corinthian church (I Corinthians 7) seven deals with a few of the many problems the church faced. Fornication was a big problem that plagued Corinth. Sexual sins slowly crept into the church. They gradually sneaked into the home causing tremors in its very foundation, threatening its very existence.

Fornication must be avoided. It can be avoided. Paul provides a simple solution by giving one great tip to help avoid this ravaging sin called fornication. He gives his one valuable advice in I Corinthians 7: 2, "Nevertheless, to avoid fornication, let every man have his own wife, and let every woman have her own husband." Paul did not go the psychiatrist to find a reasonable solution. He did not approach the psychologist. He simply turned to God for the answer. He found a Scriptural solution. The Bible provides a very simple, yet, very effective solution to combat any sin, especially fornication. In the same book, in chapter 13, Paul outlines a series of other solutions to showcase some very effective adhesives, to help fortify the home. He provides a magnificent definition and outline of love. A careful study of I Corinthians 13 is a necessity at this point.

Love is one of the most wonderful attributes of God. God has given man the ability to love as well. Every human being, saved or unsaved has the capacity to love. The unsaved person's love is tarnished because his sin has not been forgiven. Believers have a greater ability to love because they are saved. They can love in greater measure, to a fuller extent because they have God dwelling within them. A saved person has experienced the love of God.

In any relationship, marriage or other, love is the key ingredient. But, love must love for love's sake. There can be no conditions to love or it isn't true love. Love never evaluates the one it loves. It does not despise the one it loves. I often ask myself, "Did I deserve to be loved by God?" No! He loved me while I was yet sinful. Once saved, God's love can now flow through the believer. The Word of God instructs him to love.

The home of a believer should be a place where the love of God thrives. It must be a place where love not only flows but overflows. In I Corinthians 12 through 14, Paul is explaining spiritual gifts. He explains the function, the form and the future of these gifts. He clarifies their intended use and explicates their misuse.

In chapter 13 of I Corinthians Paul compares spiritual gifts with love. He comes to a conclusion that love is the best of all the gifts. Love works wonderfully well in any relationship. Besides God, love is the most essential element in marriage.

If a home is to succeed, it must have this adhesive of love. Let us examine the passage mentioned above to glean every possible principle there is to use to build a strong home. Without God's help, the home will collapse. A home built on God stands secure.

A home built on God's Word will withstand the storms of life. It will stand the test of time. For this reason, I am anxious to hear what God's Word has to say. I am eager to obey its commands, to secure my home and thereby help fortify it.

LOVE: THE BIBLE WAY

Love Defined

Paul beautifully defines love in I Corinthians 13: 4-7. It is my firm belief there is no better definition of love out there. God the author of everything defines love as: "Charity suffereth long, and is kind; charity envieth not; charity vaunteth not itself, is not puffed up, Doth not behave itself unseemly, seeketh not her own, is not easily provoked, thinketh no evil; Rejoiceth not in iniquity, but rejoiceth in the truth; Beareth all things, believeth all things, hopeth all things, endureth all things."

No better definition of love can be found in any other book in the world. The Bible alone gives us such a complete, clear, and comprehensive definition of love. This definition is like an onion. To fathom the full meaning of it, each layer must be peeled, one by one. May we begin this operation, so as to comprehend its meaning to the fullest extent.

The word used for "suffereth long" is *makrothymei*. *Matthew Henry's Commentary* elucidates,

> It can endure evil, injury, and provocation, without being filled with resentment, indignation, or revenge. It makes the mind firm, gives it power over the angry passions, and furnishes it with a persevering patience, that shall rather wait and wish for the reformation of a brother than fly out in resentment of his conduct. It will put up with many slights and neglects from the person it loves, and wait long to see the kindly effects of such patience on him.[7]

Love suffers long

Marriage is an adjustment between two strangers in most cases. Even if two people know each other for a while, it is not the same as living together after marriage. There must be a give and take attitude. To suffer long means to bear with one another. Love must suffer long if a home is to survive and thrive. God has borne up with all man's hurtful doings for about six thousand years. Man failed God miserably, shattered His dreams, and even disappointed Him. Yet, God is long suffering toward him. Praise God, His love suffers long. As children of God, we too must follow God's lead. The husband must be willing to suffer long. He must be patient. He must not give up on his partner no matter how much he may have to endure, in order to make it work.

Love is Kind

The Greek word for "kind" is *crhsteuetai* means, "tender and compassionate in itself." Adam Clark's commentary describes the attribute of kindness well, "It is tender and compassionate in itself, and kind and obliging to others; it is mild, gentle, and benign; and, if called to suffer, inspires the sufferer with the most amiable sweetness, and the most tender affection. It is also submissive to all the dispensations of God; and creates trouble to no one. Love is kind."[8]

Opportunities for fractious situations are far too numerous, within the walls of a home. To avoid friction, the home must be lubricated with kindness. Kindness averts anger. It soothes any heat in the home. It is really difficult to react negatively to kindness. Jesus was kind to people. His kindness was expressed by his compassionate reaction to the most hurtful, cruel and undeserving people. Kindness is a much-needed character for a marriage to work smoothly. It is a quality both partners must develop. Fostering an attribute such as this will help reap great dividends in the home.

Love Envieth Not

In the Greek *ou zhloi* means, "Is not grieved because another possesses a greater portion of earthly, intellectual, or spiritual blessings."[9] A love that does not envy is pure. Few can rejoice with others in their happiness, successes, comforts, and moments of honor. Paul exhorts believers to prefer others above themselves. Such love is rare. Jealousy should never be permitted or welcomed in a home. Jealousy shreds the home down. It acts like a wedge widening the distance in a relationship. It separates. The devil has used jealously as barricade to distance the husband from the wife and vice versa. Sadly, many husbands grow jealous of their wives. Many wives get jealous of their husband's success. "Jealousy" is cruel as the grave. It is a terrible sin. It is an insatiable sin, until it sees the other partner in the grave. Marriage must never be permitted to reach this phase.

Love Vaunteth Not Itself

'Vaunteth not' in the Greek is *ou perpereuetai*. "This word is variously translated; acteth not rashly, insolently; is not inconstant, & it is not agreed by learned men whether it be Greek, Latin, or Arabic. Bishop Pearce derived it from the latter language; and translates it, is not inconstant. There is a phrase in our own language that expresses what I think to be the meaning of the original, does not set itself forward-does not desire to be noticed or applauded; but wishes that God may be all in all."[10]

Love never acts rashly. Love does not seek its own praise. Love always wants to see the good of the other person. It wants to praise the other person. It is totally unselfish. This trait is worth valuing in any marriage. It will help strengthen the home.

Love is Not Puffed Up

Ou fusioutai, means "Is not inflated with a sense of its own importance; for it knows it has nothing but what it has received; and that it deserves nothing that it has got."[11] Pride is basically an attitude. As human beings, we all have some amount of pride. It is another destroyer of the home. It is of the Devil. Satan's pride caused his fall. No better illustration serves the purpose of providing caution better. Pride hinders a person from coming to God. At salvation, God's love floods the soul of the new believer. Before salvation, the sinner is at enmity with God. The believer is on the Lord's side. With God indwelling the believer, pride can be overcome with humility. Pride can be replaced with humility. Humility is necessary, if the home is to function smoothly. Where there are people, there are problems. Where there is friendship, there is great potential for friction. Humans hurt God. Humans hurt humans. Husbands hurt wives. Wives may hurt husbands. Children will hurt parents. Parents will hurt children. If you have breath in your nostrils, there will be times of discord.

During fractious moments, when strives erupt, humility can be a great appeaser. Pride keeps a person from forgiving the offender. It hinders from bringing reconciliation, resulting in bitterness. Bitterness breeds hatred. Hatred divides. Division is never constructive. It leads to disrupting the unity of the home. It intends to break up the home. Love alone can keep each partner from pride, from being puffed up or from magnifying self. So beware! Pride will surely bring you down.

Love Does Not Misbehave

Love does not behave itself in an unseemly fashion. Here, the Greek words, *ouk aschmonei*, means, love never acts out of its place. It does not misbehave in character. Love is not rude. This kind of love has to be a conscious endeavor. Treating the other partner in a polite way requires a selfless love. Jesus exemplified His pure, selfless love when He chose to die. God lost His Son in order to pay for man's sin, permitting Him to die on the cross for no wrong of His. God knew the cost of saving man. God had fully evaluated the extent of the suffering His Son had to go through. Emulating God makes it possible for each partner in marriage to have the interests of the other at heart, as a priority. Paul exemplified a selfless love when he chose to become all things to all men. Most believers fail to be vessels of flowing love. Failing to love like the way Christ loved us, puts us in a serious predicament. We cannot be instruments unto edification. Instead, we become stumbling blocks.

Love must edify

Jesus, the very God in human form, exemplified this kind of love. On a few occasions, Jesus had to be stern, but never on any occasion was Jesus ever loutish. He was not impolite to those who tried, beat, spat, or crucified Him. His first prayer was a plea to the Father. In it He asked His Father to forgive them for their sin of crucifying their very God incarnate. He said they had done it in ignorance. His love saw beyond their spiritually blind, sinfully wicked and totally depraved hearts. He loved them despite what they did to Him.

Love Is Unselfish

Love, since Adam's fall turned out to be selfish. Selfishness was one of the two original sins. It is the sin which has brought man to his present condition. It has resulted in all the consequences sin brought along with it. Selfish love is unable to satisfy God or others because it is self-centered. It seeks its own (*ou zhtei ta eauthv*). A home can never be built on such grounds. The home is designed for sharing. Every member of the home shares in all its joys or sorrows.

The home is God's design for partnership. It is a joint venture. Hence, a home can never stand alone. It must have two people, coming together to share and enjoy spiritual, bodily, physical, emotional and material pleasures. People presently, enter relationships with selfish motives. The result, the home often crumbles. The husband-wife relationship is designed for sharing. It is a spiritual relationship. Each partner ought to help the other in his/her spiritual walk with God. It is a physical relationship. It requires both giving and receiving love. Because this is a physical relationship, it suffers when the love shared is not mutual. Since this is a relationship in the flesh, it calls for the satisfying of the bodily needs of either partner. As marriage is a physical bond, it necessitates the sharing of other physical elements, such as, finances, failures, futures, and fortunes. The quality of sharing must be in practices in: success as well as failures of life; in the ups and downs of life; in sickness and in health and in plenty and in poverty. Dr. James C Dobson in his book, "Love Must Be Tough, Straight Talk" attests to man's selfishness, "There is little doubt that adolescent romance is typically selfish and introspective; it blanches and buckles when asked to sacrifice or contribute or give."[12]

Our love in a marital relationship must integrate a selfless aspect. For true love cares, shares and bears all things. Unselfish love is best exemplified in God, who gave His only begotten Son to die for a sinful world. God sacrificed His Son, so that by his death, we can all have life, life eternal. If we love like God we can love selflessly.

Love Is Not Easily Provoked

Love is not provoked (*ou paroxunetai*). True love is not easily aggravated. Controlling one's temper is a challenge these days. Reading the Bible on a daily basis and communing with God can help the believer be filled (controlled) by the Spirit. The filling of the Holy Spirit is directly related to controlling. Being "Filled" is vital for one to be able to control the natural tendencies of sin. Anger is another great destroyer of the home.

I heard this true story of a very wealthy man from Dr. Eric Franks. A rich man was materially prosperous. He was known for his kind-heartedness. One day, he got into an argument with his wife. In a moment of anger, he struck his wife on the head with the flashlight. She fell to the ground and died instantly. He had never raised his hand or struck her, in the past. Though this was the first time he struck her, it proved to be fatal. His loss turned his life tragically to a life of turmoil. He never got over what he had done to her. Missing his wife, he found a new companion in alcohol. He squandered all his money on drink. Poverty came quickly as his wealth vanished like vapor right before his eyes. His story reminds me of the danger of falling prey to being soon angered. Love is not easily provoked.

Every believer must learn to control his temper or his temper will control him. The Holy Spirit can help have victory in this vital area of our lives. We must allow the Holy Spirit control us so we can have self control.

Love Thinketh No Evil (V. 5)

The Greek has it as *oulogizetai to kakon*. Adam Clark's commentary explains this phrase,

> Never supposes that a good action may have a bad motive; gives every man credit for his profession of religion, uprightness, godly zeal, &c., while nothing is seen in

his conduct or in his spirit inconsistent with this profession. His heart is so governed and influenced by the love of God that he cannot think of evil but where it appears. The original implies that he does not invent or devise any evil; or, does not reason on any particular act or word so as to infer evil from it; for this would destroy his love to his brother; it would be ruinous to charity and benevolence.[13]

Strange, how two hearts once in love can so quickly cave in to formulate evil against each other. I say to myself, "What in the world?" Well, the depraved human heart is capable of doing the unthinkable, the unimaginable. The heart is sinful, wicked and totally depraved. Such a heart is able to produce evil. Jesus said in Mark (7:21), "For from within, out of the heart of men, proceed evil thoughts, adulteries, fornications, murders." Why blame others, for our failures. Our own wicked hearts cause us to sin. It is easy to point fingers. While pointing a finger at the other partner, remember at least three fingers point to you. Jeremiah, by divine inspiration opens up our heart, exposing its true condition. Here's what he discovered, (17:9), "The heart is deceitful above all things, and desperately wicked: who can know it?" Only God, the one who made man, knows the true potential of a wicked heart. Man does not know his own heart.

Man deceives himself if he thinks he is perfect. Pride keeps man from acknowledging his faults and failures, his sins. Real reconciliation can come only when there is real confession. In a heart surgery the doctor takes the heart out, fixes the problem, and puts the heart back. Likewise, the inner condition of each heart must be exposed.

Right diagnosis helps determine the right treatment. Before a festering wound can heal it must be cleaned. You may have to open up the wound again, to take out all the pus which is not visible on the outside. . This is painful but necessary. Marital problems must be dealt with realistically, to ensure realistic solutions. However, not every fault, sin and failure can be dealt with. The Bible does say, "Love covers a multitude of sins." We must learn to forgive forget past hurts. The blood of Jesus is able to cleanse every sin.

Understanding the heart's deceptive nature makes one realize why it is so easy to think evil thoughts and do evil acts. Yes, the heart is capable of conceiving evil even of the one you love the most. Beware! Lest you think evil about the partner God has given you. No one can stop any thought from popping up, but everyone can stop meditating on them.

Love Rejoices: not in iniquity (*ou cairei epi th adikia.*)

True love rejoices in truth and is saddened when one partner has the slightest taint of iniquity. Genuine love means loving someone like you love yourself. Unfortunately, this world consists of people who rejoice when someone: falls into sin; is down in sorrow; has a serious illness; loses a job or house. Others believe they deserve to suffer because of their wrongdoing. They are reaping what they have sown. We might think that way too saying, "Maybe, he is paying a price for his evil deeds" or "He deserves it," or "It serves him right." Can you truly rejoice, when the person you profess to love so dearly faces a dire situation, or is beaten up by some storm of life? No! No! No! In Hebrews 12:5-11 the author gives fours reasons for God's chastening. Chastening is correcting. The reasons I believe are as follows: Because we are sons; because we are to be in subjection to God; because we are corrected by God for our success or profit; and for our sanctification and His satisfaction (fruit-bearing). This is why God does not rejoice over our iniquity. He seeks to rectify our sinful condition by restoring us to fellowship. True love seeks to: restore, rebuild, rejuvenate and redeem the other. Love seeks the best for the one we love. It should never rejoice in iniquity.

Love Rejoices: In the truth

Alhyeia is the Greek word for truth. "Truth" stands in sharp contrast with anything and every thing that is opposite to falsehood. Bona fide love finds occasion to rejoice in authentic truth. Believing in the truth means, it is worth defending. Missionaries the world over have sacrificed their lives because they know what they believed and lived for is the truth.

Love rejoices in the truth because truth does not hide anything from the one it loves. It is transparent. Truth is an attribute of God. Thus, truth must be promoted, allowed to permeate and propagate itself to all people. John 14: 6 reveals the embodiment of all truth, "Jesus saith unto him, I am the way, the truth, and the life: no man cometh unto the Father, but by me." He is the true embodiment of all truth." He also made this great statement in the same book, (8:32),

"And ye shall know the truth, and the truth shall make you free." Jesus openly spoke about hell not to scare people, but to keep them from going there to spend eternity. He loved the world genuinely. He did not show forth His love through mere words, but went the whole distance, proving it with his actions. He loved enough to die, so every one that believes in Him may live. Truth ushers in the greatest freedom of all, freedom from sin. Love rejoices only in the right, only in the truth.

Love Bears All Things (V.7a)

"Beareth all things" in the Greek language are expressed by the words *"panta stegei."* The Adam Clark's commentary illuminates the bearing this phrase carries. It says, "This word is also variously interpreted: to endure, bear, sustain, cover, conceal, contain."[14] It carries the idea of cover or contain. Love does not expose or endanger the one loved. Joseph protected Mary's reputation when she carried the Lord Jesus Christ in her womb. She was a virgin. Joseph was only betrothed to her. He was not yet married. He was shocked when Mary told him she was with child. He was a man of integrity. He thought of putting her away privily, but the angel clarified matters. He still could have dissolved the situation, disrupted Mary's reputation, but he determined to stand by her.

Love covers the one it loves

In a marital relationship, love covers the sins of the other partner. Covering a multitude of sins does not mean the person is saying, wrong is right and right is wrong. In John 4, Jesus did not condemn the woman taken in adultery; neither did He condone her wrongdoing. He exhorted her to go and sin no more. Such an act provides a person the opportunity to repent. It permits the person to a privilege to reconcile. It gives the person a second chance, allowing the individual to start afresh. Peter writes on similar lines (1 Pet 4:8), "And above all things have fervent charity among yourselves: for charity shall cover the multitude of sins." True love does rebuke, but it does so with kindness, while yet providing the person protection and security.

Love Believeth All Things (*Panta pisteuei*: v. 7b)

Love readily trusts. It anticipates the best, expects the best. The antonym of trust is doubt. A lack of trust is the root cause of doubt. Love readily believes. To trust means to express confidence in the other person. When doubts arise, one partner must let the other the have the benefit of the doubt. Satan brings doubts into relationships. He caused Adam and Eve to doubt God's warning. He raises many questions. If both parties in a marriage maintain clear lines of communication, doubt can be kept at bay.

Communication requires honesty. It demands transparency. Clear communication helps build bridges in marriage. Someone said, "Trust begets trust." This is a true statement. Living a life of honesty builds a network of trust. It fosters trust in our partners. Love does believe all things.

Love Hopeth All Things (*Panta elpizei*: v.7c)

When the image of a person is fully tarnished, Paul says true love can still find something to hope for in a faltering individual. It never gives up. A love that hopes is not a love that covers up the wrong. But, it is a love which looks for anything positive to encourage the person hoping he will make it. Hope gives the individual a second chance. It gives another opportunity to repent. Hope gives a person another chance to turn to God.

Our great God is a God of second chances. In Isaiah 42: 3, God demonstrates His love and hope for a person on his last limb if you will by saying, "A bruised reed shall he not break, and the smoking flax shall he not quench: he shall bring forth judgment unto truth." God's immutable nature in this regard is visible in the New Testament Scripture passage of Romans 5: 20, "Moreover the law entered, that the offence might abound. But where sin abounded, grace did much more abound." Aren't you glad our God is a God of second chances? Such a love draws men to repentance.

Once repentance has been achieved, the person can be restored completely to all of the privileges which can be enjoyed by a believer, reestablishing fellowship in every other area of life. The home must be a place where such love is displayed. No individual within the walls of the home should ever lose hope. Let us earnestly endeavor to see the good in our spouses and our kids.

Love Endureth All Things

Sometimes in relationships, false accusations stem from uncanny sources. Job found his closest friends accused him. He calls them "miserable comforters." Their wrong attitude did not give Job the license to grumble, complain or curse God. To further worsen his misery, his dear wife suggested, it was better for Job to curse God and die. But Job endured his share of trials. His grit and determination to endure his cross made him come out victorious. He did not get angry with his wife. He endured his trials, his tormenting friends and his taunting wife. Love endures all things for love's sake. If we truly love our spouse, we will be able to endure every difficulty, every trial coming our way. Such love cannot lose. It will triumph. Jesus endured the shame, the reproach and pain from Gethsemane all the way to Golgotha. He endured the shame His cruel criticizers caused him from the court rooms to Calvary. He saw their sadness though He heard their shouts "Crucify Him, crucify Him." He soothed the hearts of the wailing women, while weeping within for the wounded souls of men who would waste in a hell. He endured all things because He genuinely loved all of mankind. He painted a perfect picture of endurance. True love endures all things.

Love Never Fails

Charity never faileth (*'h agaph oudepote ekpiptei*). Paul places great value of exercising love. Comparing all the spiritual gifts, Paul says, "Charity never faileth: but whether there be prophecies, they shall fail; whether there be tongues, they shall cease; whether there be knowledge, it shall vanish away." Love has the ability to provide every relationship the security and drive necessary to take it to the finish line.

Love seeks to preserve relationships. Love values relationships that matter most in our lives. The order of our relationships must be: first God, then those within the home. The Bible is God's love letter to man. In it, God penned down the reason why He sent His only Son. It was the most visible way for God to express His sincere love for man.

Love is God's greatest gift to us. It is the greatest gift we posses. It we use it to our benefit, it will help our relationship succeed. Love does not give up on the one it loves. Love is an investment of all we have. It was an incalculable investment on God's part. It cost God His Son, His solidarity and His severance of His eternal relationship. Love is costly.

Love never faileth the one in whom it has vested interests. So, knowing for a fact we have a faithful, loving God on our side and love in our hearts, the home can be kept from crumbling. Such love cannot fail.

LOVE'S ROLES AND RESPONSIBILITIES

EPHESIANS 5: -33

Love is one of the most precious, wonderful gifts God has given us. A beautiful picture of love cannot be painted if we exclude God from the portrait. The love of God is rich and full. His love is worth emulating. The love of Jesus drew men unto Himself. He made people feel worth. In our Christian lives we must endeavor to love like Christ. It is an asset sure to yield rich dividends. No other love compares to the love of Christ. His is a pure, precious and perfect love. Has the love of Christ ever made you wonder? It has puzzled me. I have often wondered "How could He love a wretch like me?" His love has made me ask with awestruck bewilderment, "Why He chooses to love a sinner such as me?" Notice the words of the song, "If That Isn't love," presented below. In it the author tries to express God's love which transcends all boundaries and barriers. He tries to articulate His love which surpasses words and translates into action. In the lyrics the song writer tries to find words to express this wonderful love. He writes,

> He left the splendor of heaven
> Knowing His destiny
> Was the lonely hill of Golgotha
> There to lay down His life for me And if that isn't love
> Then the ocean is dry

There's no stars in the sky
And the little sparrows can't fly
Yeah if that isn't love
Then heaven's a myth
There's no feeling like this
If that isn't love

Even in death He remembered
The thief hanging by His side
Then he spoke of love and compassion
And He took him to paradise

And if that isn't love
Then the ocean is dry
There's no stars in the sky
And the little sparrows can't fly
Yeah if that isn't love
Then heaven's a myth
There's no feeling like this
If that isn't love

Paul bequeaths valuable advice for three kinds of relationships in the book of Ephesians. In Chapter 5.22 through 6: 9, he explains the roles and responsibilities of each. The roles and responsibilities of: the husband and wife (Eph 5:22-33), parent and child (Eph 6:1-4), master and servant (Eph 6:4-9) are all explained in these verses. Since the Word of God sheds light on these vital roles, and on all other matters, the Psalmist proclaims (Ps 119:105), "Thy word is a lamp unto my feet, and a light unto my path." How vital for the finite creature to seek the Infinite's wisdom and will on matters! Examining this passage of Scripture clarifies our understanding of the roles God wants us to play as partners in a home. Fulfilling our part of the role will aid making the building proper.

Ephesians 5: 22-6-4 is a portion of Scripture which details the relationships within the home. Paul addresses the wives first. Roles are God-given. This is the first lesson we must learn in regard to God-given roles. This eliminates choice. Not only are our roles given by God. He has given us a command to perform the responsibilities attached to these roles. Each individual has the responsibility to fulfill his role effectively. Performing our God-given role enables the God-given relationship to thrive. Thrive is the key word here, not strive. Strife is the undesired outcome when we fail to carry out our roles correctly. Much like an orchestra, each individual instrument must play in harmony in order to produce good, sweet music. Every musician has his music sheet, his instrument, his talent and training. However good an individual musician might be, a good orchestra is never a one-man show. It is not a solo performance. In an orchestra every musician must synchronize his or her part with the whole group. When perfect harmony is achieved, great music is produced. The two individuals in a marital union must work together, to slowly but surely synchronize their individual talents and traits for the total benefit of the home. The sooner such synchrony is achieved, the faster success can be attained.

Women Are To Submit

Compliance can be commanded but it will fail to fortify companionship. Submission must come by willing surrender to a God-given role. Submission may seem hard to come by when it is viewed as an inferior position. The fact of the matter however reinstates the reality that submission is not a matter of a lower position but a loftier synchronism. Learning this vital lesson helps us not shy away from submission. Wives ought to submit to their own husbands (v. 22). How must they submit? The Bible says, "As unto the Lord." God provides a comparison. He gives a pattern to follow. How must she be subject? Just as the church is subject unto Christ, she ought to be subject to her own husband. To what extent must she be submissive? The Bible says, "In everything."

Women's rights movement directly opposes Biblical truths. Their opposition to a God-given mandate has only led to the collapse of the home. Obviously, collapse of the home is inevitable when one ignores God's omniscient orders. Women must realize submission is not man's concept. Man did not invent this idea to rule over women. It was God's idea. It is His design. Submission makes the home run smoothly and efficiently.

The home is collapsing for many reasons. One of them is because women have failed to conform to God's command. They fail to comply to and heed God's caution. Instead, women have assumed a different role. A role God has not designed. Assuming such a role always brings opposition and oppression. It robs the home of God's blessing and is bound to breed contentions and strife. Such a home struggles to stand strong.

Husbands are to lead like Christ

God gave man the responsibility to be the head of the home (v. 23). He is to lead. His role as leader is also mandated by God. God gave man a pattern to follow, so he can perform his role very well, the way God intended. How is man to lead his wife, his home? He must lead the way Christ leads the church. Just as Christ is the head of the church, man is the head of the home. Just as Christ is the savior of the body, man is responsible to salvage his family from every threat and trial. The idea of 'savior of the body' pertains to the fact that Jesus saved the Church by His substitutionary death on the cross. The husband's role as savior of the home, I believe has to do with guarding it with all of his resources. He must guard the home at all costs. He must safeguard the home from every possible threat or attack.

Husbands are to love like Christ (v. 25)

Men are generally not good at loving their wives. They have to work at it. A man can love his work naturally because he is designed for work. He was not originally designed to love another human being. For this reason, God instructs the husband to love his wife. What is the pattern or standard by which he is to love his wife? He must love his wife, just as Christ loved the church. To what extent must he love? He must love to the extent of even giving his life for her. How must he love his wife? He is to love his wife as his own body (v. 28). Why does God want a man to love his wife as his own body? The reason, no man hates his own body. This implies the wife is part and parcel of her husband. They are one flesh. Man must take his responsibility to love his wife seriously. The seriousness of his role is emphasized three times (vv. 25, 28, and 33) within the span of a few short verses.

When love prevails, the home cannot fail. God is interested in preserving the home. The home is His divine design. Will God's pattern succeed? In the book "Love Life" written by Ed Wheat, there is a frightening statistic: "More than one million divorces will split American households this year. About 75 percent of the family units in this country will need counseling help at some time. At least 40 percent of all married couples will divorce eventually." If this is true, is God's plan working out? Will God's plan succeed? Yes, it will. You may ask, 'How?' God's plan will work, simply because He is God and He says so. God is doing His part but another question must be asked. Is man doing his part?

God's is omniscient. His omniscience enables Him to see the end from the beginning. He sees it all. He knows what works best and what won't. Why try something new? Trust God and follow His Word. By acting in faith and in obedience we can build a home that is sure, secure and solid. Rock Solid! Do you realize how important it is to have God in our plans, in our design, and in the development of the home? How can we ever build a home and build it well without Him. The Psalmist sees the futility of building a home without God. He knows the danger. Any home built on the sand, will fall. Any home built on anything other than God, will fall. Thus the Psalmist (Psalm 127:1) concretely concludes by saying, "Except the LORD build the house, they labour in vain that build it: except the LORD keep the city, the watchman waketh but in vain." Let the LORD build your home and mine! Everyone must arrive at the very same conclusion, if the home is to succeed.

CHAPTER TEN

I COULDN'T HAVE DONE IT WITHOUT HIM

I DARED TO RIDE

Knott's Berry Farm, 2007, the first time I ever rode a roller coaster. Memories flash back of how my wife and kids coaxed me to get one of the many frightening rides. I am fearful of heights. Levels of thrill or danger were marked at the entrance of each ride. I was clueless about these ratings, hence unaware of the fear factor involved. I did not want my family to think "I was a chicken," so I sat down in my seat. Though my heart was racing, I pretended to be brave and strong. The next sound I heard distinctly was the sound of my seat belt. I heard it "click" and lock into place. The count down began, five, four, three, two, one, and I was shot like a stone from a catapult, like an arrow from a bow. When the ride was done, I felt like I still was in motion. My hair looked like a porcupine's quills. Reminiscing about it, now, from the comfort of the couch in my living room, I guess I actually did enjoy the ride, after all. At least for one special reason, it made my family happy.

Long, long ago, fourteen years ago to be precise, I embarked on a wonderful journey. It was November 3rd, 1993, after much prayer, I decided to ask Leah, if she would consider being my wife. It was Christmas Eve 1994, close to midnight, she finally replied to my proposal.

It was a forty-minute drive back home from Church. My feet pressed hard on the accelerator pedal. I was nervous, because I had in my hand, Leah's reply to my question, "Will you consider being my wife?" I was not afraid what the reply possibly was, but I was nervous. I had prayed about God's will for my life for a long enough time. I felt the peace of God in my heart.

Excitement was in the air. It was the season of Christmas. People were walking back home from Christmas Eve services. Many churches in India had mid night services. There was joy all around. I was anxious to get home. But, no matter how hard I tried to get home that night, the drive seemed to take forever. All the way home my mind paced like a deer. Mixed emotions, thoughts, even a quick dart of doubt shot across my mind. I shunned the thought, "What if?" Um, it doesn't matter. It's all in God's hands," I realized.

MOMENTS OF SUSPENSE

I was in love, I really was. But was she in love with me? This is the big question. These forty minutes or so seemed to take forever.

These were the slowest moments of my life. It seemed as though the clock had forgotten to tick. It looked like the hands of the clock had frozen to a halt. After dropping off all my Church members who accompanied me to the watch night service, I was finally headed home. When I got home, I now can't recall how I parked my car that day. I don't recollect whether I even turned off the engine or not. It didn't matter. I do remember this part of the story. I literally ran the ten feet or so to my front door. Scrambling with Leah's gift in my hand, I finally began opening up her gift. My parents were puzzled why I behaved so weirdly that day. Only I knew the reason. The final verdict, her decision was in my hands, inside her gift. To say the least, I can spell her answer. It was a three-letter word. The little English word, "Yes," was her reply. Yes! She had agreed to be my wife. What a perfect time to add to the festivity already in the air. Joy flooded my soul.

THE BEST CHRISTMAS GIFT EVER

Apart from the Lord Jesus Christ, this was the best Christmas gift I had ever received. I did not know how to respond to this beautiful, wonderful gift. I did not know whether to run around the block, shout for joy, or cry. Boy! I was so thrilled. All I could do for the moment was thank God. I said, "Thank you Jesus, thank you." I had found my helpmeet. I had found my one-true love. Looking back, I wonder, "What did Leah like in me?" I had nothing extraordinary to offer her. I was just a sinner, saved by Grace. I did not have a job, no wealth, nothing outstanding for her to be attracted to me. I was still a student at Calvary Baptist Bible College and Seminary. These were special days though, days wherein, all I had was God. God was sufficient, more than sufficient. Now, I had Leah to travel this pilgrim journey of life, along with me.

The overwhelming joy did not last for long. The road from thereon was not going to be easy. My journey was much like the roller coaster ride. Since, the first ride in Knott's Berry Farm, I have been on numerous other rides. I have been on rides in Disney Land's theme park (Disney's California Adventure Park). What fun, fear, and facial expressions it brought. Much like these rides, my life has had its share of good and bad times. I have faced many ups and downs. I have been on some mountain top experiences. I have been down in the valley, just like when the roller coaster darted down at a deadly pace. It wound this way and that, so my life's journey has meandered. In all, I can say it has been a good ride.

Looking back, I see very thankfully how God's hand orchestrated my life. Some memories bring joy, others tears. Some recollections bring some sadness, yet we can see God's grace has helped us. Through it all, we can gratefully say, we have made it thus far.

The lyrics of the song, "Through it All" express our life's journey, wonderfully well. I can join the author in singing with much appreciation the words he penned down:

I've had many tears and sorrows,
I've had questions for tomorrow,
There've been times I didn't know right from wrong:
But in every situation God gave blessed consolation
That my trials come to only make me strong.

Through it all, through it all,
I've learned to trust in Jesus,
I've learned to trust in God;
Through it all, through it all,
I've learned to depend upon His Word.

I've been to lots of places,
And I've seen a lot of faces,
There've been times I felt so all alone;
But in my lonely hours,
Yes, those precious lonely hours,
Jesus let me know that I was His own.

Through it all, through it all,
I've learned to trust in Jesus,
I've learned to trust in God;
Through it all, through it all,
I've learned to depend upon His Word.

I thank God for the mountains,
And I thank Him for the valleys,
I thank Him for the storms
He brought me through;
For if I'd never had a problem
I wouldn't know that He could solve them,
I'd never know what faith in God could do.

Through it all, through it all,
I've learned to trust in Jesus,
I've learned to trust in God;
Through it all, through it all,
I've learned to depend upon His Word.[1]

Our struggles and successes don't mean a thing if it wasn't for God. We cannot glory in our triumphs. God has been extremely good. His grace did help us make it through each day. Through it all, we've learned to depend upon the Lord. Through all these situations God brought us close to Him and His precious Word. All credit goes to God. His gracious hand has led us thus far, and will safely lead us home. God who faithfully saved us has also secured our salvation and our home. He has anchored my family and my home.

THE AMAZING GRACE OF GOD

I cannot do justice to this work, if I don't both declare and admit the work of God's grace in our lives, especially in mine. I'd like to confess, we have fed off the grace of God. Had it not been for the grace of God, I would never have been saved, I would not have a wife, a home or kids. I am so blessed to have the tiniest blessing I now possess. I like to make my God look great. I want to magnify Him. In all truth, this is not flattery or falsity. I want to talk of His grace. It is by His grace I have lived. Though the Lord has taken us through many phases in our fleeting life, He has piloted me well.

Let me tell you the story of the song "Amazing Grace." John Vassar penned the lyrics of this soul-stirring song. Vassar was a great soul winner for Christ. He went from door to door distributing tracts and talking with people about the Lord Jesus and their souls.

One woman heard about him, and his desperate attempt to knock on every door. She determined to slam the door on his face, if he came to her home. He did come by the next day. There was a ring on her doorbell. Identifying Vassar by the description she had received, she followed her well thought out plan through. She slammed the door on his face. John Vassar did not despair, but sat down on her doorstep and sang these heart-touching words:

> But drops of grief can ne'er repay
> The debt of love I owe,
> Here, Lord, I give myself away;
> 'Tis all that I can do.[2]

The woman heard the tone of his earnest voice, listened to the sincerity of the words he sang, was deeply convicted by it. She quickly opened the door, called Mr. Vassar in, and God's grace saved her on that glorious day.

Amazing Grace!

> (1) Amazing grace! How sweet the sound-
>   That saved a wretch like me!
>   I once was lost but now am found,
>   Was blind but now I see.

> (2) 'Twas grace that taught my heart to fear,
>   And grace my fears relieved:
>   How precious did that grace appear
>   The hour I first believed!

(3) The Lord has promised good to me,

> His word my hope secures;
>
> He will my shield and portion be
>
> As long as life endures.

(4) Through many dangers, toils, and snares,

> I have already come;
>
> 'Tis grace hath brought me safe thus far,
>
> And grace will lead me home.

(4) When we've been there ten thousand years,

> Bright shining as the sun,
>
> We've no less days to sing God's praise
>
> Than when we'd first begun.[3]

What glorious words! What a wonderful song! God's grace is truly amazing indeed. I do thank God for the day He found me. I was a wretched sinner. I deserved to go to hell. I deserved all of God's punishment. Thankfully, God's amazing grace did find and save me. It was my best day of my life.

My next best day came on May 7, 1994. At 4: 30 p.m. that day, I made my second most important decision. I took Leah to be my lawfully wedded wife. I stood amazed when my eyes caught a glimpse of my beautiful bride, standing at the entrance of the All

Saints Church in Richmond Town, Bangalore, India. I was ecstatic, thrilled, and overjoyed.

The day, I so longed for, had finally arrived. It was on the auspicious day, I started a joint-venture, partnering with God to begin "a great work," a work of grace entirely. I began a project called "PROJECT HOME." The engagement ring I had gifted Leah has three precious stones. Leah asked me, "Richy, why did you choose three stones on the ring." I answered, "Because it represents, God, you and me. It was given in anticipation of beginning my dream project, "PROJECT HOME."

MY FIRST PIT STOP

The thrill of driving a racing car is hard to put down in words. It is hard to describe. The ride is exciting, the rush of adrenaline, too awesome. The thrill may be worth the risks but there are very real dangers involved. I had managed to win Leah's approval to be my bride. This meant one battle has been won. But there were more battles to be won, for Leah to become my wife. I thank God for battles, so long as I don't have to fight them. I am so thankful to God I am a Christian. I am so glad I am on the Lord's side. Since He is the stronger one in our partnership, I let him fight all of my battles. Paul had this to say concerning his battle (thorn) in the flesh (II Cor. 12:7-10), "And lest I should be exalted above measure through the abundance of the revelations, there was given to me a thorn in the flesh, the messenger of Satan to buffet me, lest I should be exalted above measure. For this thing I besought the Lord thrice, that it might depart from me." Paul had some serious battles to fight. Thankfully, he could rely on God to take the lead, to help fight his battles.

One powerful, secret weapon was part of my armory which gave me a lot of confidence. It was weapon like none other. I needed it to help me overcome all the many hurdles before I could get to the wedding altar. It did help me win the victories. This was not a weapon of my invention. It was a God given tool I could use when ever I was in dire straights. I used it to help me many times. Jesus used it while on earth to communicate with His heavenly Father.

The weapon of prayer is a wonderful artillery God has given to every believer. It is readily available for use anytime, anywhere. It is a tool that gets us to God. It helps us stay in touch with our Creator. It establishes the communication line to seek the divine architect's help any time we need it. It is an always open access line, never busy or engaged.

There are some things about prayer we need to keep in mind when we get in touch with God. Prayer helps us communicate with Him. However, it does not guarantee His approval on all we ask or seek. An all-wise God sometimes sees fit to delay or deny our prayers. Paul experienced God's denial first hand in a dire situation of his life. He requested God to take away a thorn in his flesh. What ever the thorn, it made Paul's life uncomfortable and inconvenient. In response to his plea God's reply came in these words. Paul pens them down for our benefit (VV.9-10), "And he said unto me, My grace is sufficient for thee: for my strength is made perfect in weakness. Most gladly therefore will I rather glory in my infirmities, that the power of Christ may rest upon me. Therefore I take pleasure in infirmities, in reproaches, in necessities, in persecutions, in distresses for Christ's sake: for when I am weak, then am I strong."

Victory number one had just been won. It was the victory of having Leah agreeing to marry me. I had other battles to fight. There were battles I had to face on my own. Leah would have to face her share of them but God was faithful. He fought for us and won many victories on our behalf. Some victories were big, others small. They are victories nonetheless. I asked God to help me fight my battles. He did.

One of my first battles was, in my new endeavor to get to the altar was to tell Leah's parents of my intentions of marrying her. I did set an appointment to talk to them, but when the time came my heart fluttered like a butterfly. Whispering a prayer, I said, "Lord will you please help me through this?" "Help me! Help me; give me the right words to say." At the meeting, I announced my intentions for Leah saying, "I am in love with your daughter Leah. It is not mere friendship that I seek. I want to marry her." Leah's dad said he was happy for us, and would pray about this. Her mom was not fully convinced I was the right man for her daughter. She wondered if Leah was making the right decision. It was not easy for Leah's dad either to hear of his favorite daughter's proposal for marriage. This was a big deal for me, my first storm. Though their answer was not an affirmative "Yes!" it did not mean a "No" either. To me, this was a victory. God had helped me face a tough day in my life. I did get to meet Leah's parents, and God gave me the boldness to clearly indicate my intentions for their daughter. One more battle had been fought, and one more victory had been won.

I had survived two battles. I had overcome a few mountains. These were just the beginning stages of my long road to the altar ahead. A new battle would surface soon. A new hurdle would be in my way. I had to overcome them. The important thing was to stay focused. I had to visualize the day I would finally stand at the altar, see my bride, and hear the two little words loud and clear, "I do." It was this vision that kept me going. I knew I could make it because God was with me to help me each step of the way.

Now that I had indicated my intentions to Leah's parents, I had to get my parents approval and favor. When I got back home that day, I was both happy and nervous. Mixed feelings, like surfing waves, bobbed up and down. Suppertime came around. There was an unusual silence at the supper table. An eerie feeling filled the air. It's strange how close you can get to God when you need His help. I stayed both in touch and in tune with Him during these days. I was conscious about needing Him, seeking His consensus in all I did. I muttered a quick prayer in my mind, "Lord, here's one more battle you have to help me with." I was happy I did not want to be secretive about my desires. I did not want my parents to discover my relationship with Leah. I wanted them to be part and parcel of all my life's events. It was good that way. I am sure God was pleased with my plan. I was their child. They had invested their time, money, and energies on me. I owed them my honesty. They were special. They needed to know. I had to tell them what was on my mind. I needed their approval and blessing.

It was hard to eat that night. I felt an unusual lump in my throat. I just had to get my thoughts off my chest for any food to go down that night. Like Moses, I stammered. Coughing up some words, I said, "Mom, Dad, do you like Leah?" Don't you think it is a strange way to being a conversation? Never had this kind of a topic surfaced in our home. My parents knew Leah's family for a while and even liked them. They were taken aback wondering why I even mentioned Leah's name in this conversation. They looked at me strangely, not saying a word. I think they all choked on their food. Sensing the silence, I took a deep breath. Then, I continued to my next statement, "I love Leah and I want to marry her." It was like a bomb had been dropped. The weight had been lifted off my chest. I had spilled the words out on the table. Shocked and surprised, all our thoughts and emotions were out of whack that night. My brothers were speechless. The talk of another woman entering our family of men was unthinkable. For the past twenty-five years or so, my mom was the only lady at home. I had two brothers, thus we were four men and one lady, in all. That was not the problem. A love marriage was not too acceptable in our Indian custom. Usually, parents found a suitable girl to be a prospective bride. They would study the family background, educational level of the girl, and spiritual stand. If the girl had met their expectation, they discussed the matter with the higher ranks in the family (Grandparents, uncles and aunts). It was only after these all this, the boy would get to see the girls picture. He did not have a say in the matter.

I had broken some traditional barriers in my home. I had left the traditional Church of England of which I was a member since childhood. I had joined Calvary Baptist Bible College and Theological Seminary. Now I had brought my own proposal. I wished they would consider this proposal a good one. I hoped they would approve my choice and pick Leah to soon become my bride. Well, I had at least let the cat out of the bag. With God's help, I had spelled out my thoughts. Now, I thought it best, to let the dust settle down. So, I deliberately avoided talking about Leah for a few days.

Soon, God worked things out. Dates for our engagement and wedding were set. The rest is history. I just can't pass up this opportunity without telling you, this one story and song. I'll briefly explain an event that took place before my engagement. A British gentleman had become part of our family. Alexander Benjamin Walker claimed us to be his family, so he was part of everything we did. He was almost like a grandfather to me. Hearing of my engagement, he gave me his black suit. For some reason, I did not like the idea of a black suit but I did not have a choice. So, I took it to a tailor to alter it to fit me. To make matters worse, the tailor messed up the pant. Getting my foot through the pant was like getting into the spacesuit of an astronaut. I am not complaining about the situation but just sharing the strange happenings in my life. The suit did not stop me from getting to my engagement. Nothing mattered so long as I could place an engagement ring and later a wedding ring on Leah's finger. My thoughts drifted from the suit to the ring I had purchased for my Leah, reminding me of a sweet love song I had sung often without any meaning. Now, all of a sudden it made so much sense. I managed to find and download the lyrics of this song from the website "Actionext." The words of the song read:

> She wears my ring to show the world
> That she belongs to me
> She wears my ring to tell the world
> She's mine eternally
> With loving care
> I placed it on her finger
> To show my love
> For all the world to see
> This tiny ring is a token
> Of tender emotion
> And in this pool of love
> That's as deep as the ocean
> She swears to wear it
> With eternal devotion
> That's why I sing
> Because she wears my ring
> This tiny ring is a token
> Of tender emotion
> And in this pool of love
> That's as deep as the ocean
> She swears to wear it
> With eternal devotion

That's why I sing
Because she wears my ring
That's why I sing
Because she wears my ring[4]

These are wonderful memoirs. The ring is only a shadow of the real thing. It does nothing but remind of the promise I made to my wife on my wedding day in 1994. I would never lose my relationship with my wife if I lost the ring. Now I've grown in my walk with the Lord. These songs are a thing of the past. Spiritual songs have taken up all the space in my heart since then, replacing the music, melody and lyrics of the world.

God had brought me a long way in my relationship. Looking back, I recall the walk down the narrow, rugged path when I first gave Leah my proposal card. I remember the day I got engaged. I reminisce the day I got married. Treasured moments of my past, each of these events seem as if they happened just yesterday. I muse of the day I began my joint-venture with God. What a journey this has been! I wish I could go back in time, live those days once more. They are history now. These are wonderful stories, I can tell my grandchildren some day. However, there are days ahead of me. Days where I can make memories, build a rich legacy. Have some great stories I can leave behind. I still am building my home, and so is God.

Fourteen years into construction, my home is getting better. It is being built with God own gracious hand. He is molding me, shaping my home, and building every member of it, brick by brick. He will complete it one day and perfect it to fit His flawless blue print and design. When complete, it will be as perfect as He had meant it to be. I could never build my home the way God can. All glory be to God. I could never have come this far without Him. I couldn't have done it without Him. Can you?

CHAPTER ELEVEN

AS FOR ME AND MY HOME

Partnering with God, to build my home has turned out to be, the best project ever. Building a home isn't easy. It takes time, energy, investments, and all you've got. Accomplishing such a gigantic, mammoth-task needs help. God's help. We need to constantly stay in touch with God, so we can communicate with Him and be on the same page as Him. Prayer is a powerful tool that enables us to stay in touch with the Master Craftsman, the Chief Architect of our home, God. A book entitled, "Help In Troubled Times" by Bruce E. Mills has a nice poem describing the value seeking God's help and the importance of building the family altar:

> There are pure golden links that bind all families
> Who kneel together for a time of prayer,
> And always in their midst an unseen presence
> Waits to bless them there;
>
> Waits with outstretched arms and hands to gather
> Them close to him: these one whose altars rise

Beside a lighted lamp, a glowing fire-
And oh, how very wise
Are they who take Christ in consideration;
Who turn to him for guidance and for strength;
Who take him for a friend to walk beside them
A lifetime's length

We have Christ's promise that he will be with them:
"Where two or three are gathered-there I will
Be in their midst..." Almost we hear the echo
Of his footsteps on the still,
Entering to keep his vital promise,
Entering to be their sacred guest,
Dear Lord, may every member of these families
Find thy peace, thy rest.[1]

I never regret collaborating with God in the pursuit of building my home. The idea of the home comes straight from His heart. The home is His design, His desire and His doing. Three down to earth things (D's) must be done if you would like to partner with God on this great project. They are: decision, dependence, and durability. We have been through a few triangles. We have seen its strength. Let's review a few. God Himself exists as a triangle. The Godhead consists of: God the Father, God the Son, and God the Spirit. The home can stand strong if it stands on this triangle. Then we passed by the triangle forming the foundation on which the home is built. Let's remember, the home is built on God, God's Word and God's church. Finally, we see how a godly home may be established. This triangle that consists of: decision, dependence and durability. It will help complete the home and glorify God, its founder.

DECISION

The first step in building a home begins with the desire to build it to glorify God. This decision has to be made by individually. Towards the end of Joshua's life, he still made the commitment to walk with God. He chose God willfully, making a public confession of his decision. Here's how he carefully words it (Joshua 24: 15), "And if it seem evil unto you to serve the LORD, choose you this day whom ye will serve; whether the gods which your fathers served that were on the other side of the flood, or the gods of the Amorites, in whose land ye dwell: but as for me and my house, we will serve the LORD."

Joshua has to be commended for his great choice. Choosing God is always a wise choice. Men ought to make such decisions. Husband, you need to choose God. Wife, you need to choose God. Child, you need to choose God. Every family must choose God. Homes must choose God. Every individual in the home must make God his or her choice for salvation and life. Wise choices are wonderful choices when they are based on God and God's Word. Such choices guarantee a wise walk through the rugged, fleeting and finite life. Have you chosen to partner with God?

DEPENDANCE

Man could not survive happily for long all by himself. Despite all other creatures Adam had to live with in the Garden of Eden, he felt very lonely. God graciously met his need for a helpmeet and home by making a woman, Eve. Likewise, no individual can enjoy life alone for a prolonged period of time. Those who try to do so live very lonely lives. They are the most miserable people of all. Talking of salvation, man cannot attain it on his own. No individual can independently attain salvation by depending on his own effort or even try to earn it. Every human being ever saved, is saved by faith alone, through grace alone. Every person is saved by God alone. The reason I bring salvation in here is because salvation makes an open declaration stating one's dependence upon God.

Depending on God is not a bad choice. It is the best choice. It does not make you weak. It is the right thing to do. It makes us strong. Let me illustrate. David the shepherd boy, when he turned king, never forgot his early childhood and teenage days. Back then he was an ordinary shepherd boy. Those were boot camp days, in David's life. It was during those times, God taught Him lessons on "Dependence." His lessons on dependence were burned into his bones when, in the open fields he bluntly confronted a lion and a bear. These were valuable lessons. They would come to his aid later on in life.

On one occasion, his father sent him on an errand to deliver some goods and goodies to his brothers. While obeying his father' command, David first set eyes on the mighty Goliath. David's immediate response is an expression of the confidence he had in his God, "And David spake to the men that stood by him, saying, What shall be done to the man that killeth this Philistine, and taketh away the reproach from Israel? for who is this uncircumcised Philistine, that he should defy the armies of the living God?" David's words speak volumes of his dependence on God. He faith in God gave him a kind of confidence no other Israelite had.

No other Israelite, including King Saul dared to confront the mighty Goliath. The giant taunted the timid Israelites day and night. When Saul first heard about the young lad's willingness to fight Goliath, he shunned the idea. David tried to convince Saul he was ready to take on this challenge. Though the simple shepherd boy did not have the looks of a warrior he had an unsurpassable secret strength and confidence. He narrates some past perilous experiences through which he says, "The Lord delivered me" (v. 37). His previous experiences (I Samuel 17: 34-36) were proof of his present confidence and capability.

> And David said unto Saul, Thy servant kept his father's sheep, and there came a lion, and a bear, and took a lamb out of the flock:
> And I went out after him, and smote him, and delivered it out of his mouth: and when he arose against me, I caught him by his beard, and smote him, and slew him.
> Thy servant slew both the lion and the bear: and this uncircumcised Philistine shall be as one of them, seeing he hath defied the armies of the living God.

David's daring attitude was directly related to his dependence upon God, "the God of the armies." At the end of his life he wrote Psalm 23, talking of God's faithfulness and dependability. Verse four says, "Yea, though I walk through the valley of the shadow of death, I will fear no evil: for thou art with me; thy rod and thy staff they comfort me." The rod is something a shepherd could lean on when he was tired. It was something he could depend upon in distressing situations. At times when the poor sheep could not see the shepherd because of the thick fog, the shepherd tapped his rod on the ground assuring the sheep of his presence. David says God's presence was real to Him in every situation of his life. When you learn to depend on God, you receive God's comfort. The rod was like a hook, able to pull a sheep caught in the thicket, or a sheep fallen in a hole. It was a means of protection. The shepherd could use it as a weapon to fight an animal which threatened to take one of the sheep. It speaks of protection. The sheep could feel secure because the sound of the Shepherd's rod meant he was around, and so they were well protected. The sheep felt they could depend on the shepherd for both provision and protection. Much can be said about the "rod and staff," but we must press on.

David's ultimate confrontation with Goliath is a story that has so captivated me since I was a little boy. I am yet to meet a kid who gets tired of hearing this story. Finally, after Goliath shouted out threats to little shepherd boy, David bravely responds (I Samuel 17: 45-46), taking his staff in his hand (a reminder of his dependence upon God)

> Then said David to the Philistine, Thou comest to me with a sword, and with a spear, and with a shield: but I come to thee in the name of the LORD of hosts, the God of the armies of Israel, whom thou hast defied.
> This day will the LORD deliver thee into mine hand; and I will smite thee, and take thine head from thee; and I will give the carcases of the host of the Philistines this day unto the fowls of the air, and to the wild beasts of the earth; that all the earth may know that there is a God in Israel.

David was a stalwart of faith. Depending on God to kill Goliath, his little stone struck the fatal blow. One little stone, hurled high into the air, directed by God's own hand, brought the terrible Goliath crashing down.

Paul found great strength in depending on God. He speaks of the means by which he could do anything God wanted him to do. He says (Philippians 4:13), "I can do all things through Christ which strengtheneth me." In Romans, he tells of the fact that every believer can enjoy success because of the little pronoun "Him" in this verse (8:37), "Nay, in all these things we are more than conquerors through him that loved us." You can never go wrong when you depend entirely on God. We can build the home, the home God wants us so much to have. Learn to depend on God. It is not a sign of weakness but meekness. Learn to depend on God.

Durability

Anything God builds is durable. This little word or phrase, "For ever" speaks of durability. Let us briefly study this word. The first use of this word is found in Genesis (3: 22), "And the LORD God said, Behold, the man is become as one of us, to know good and evil: and now, lest he put forth his hand, and take also of the tree of life, and eat, and live for ever." God created Adam and Eve as eternal beings; hence, Adam's sin is eternal. To Abraham God said (Genesis 13:15), "For all the land which thou seest, to thee will I give it, and to thy seed for ever." His covenant with Abraham was that he would possess it, eternally. Israel would last forever. David's throne and kingdom will last forever (II Samuel 7:13), "He shall build an house for my name, and I will stablish the throne of his kingdom for ever. 2 Sam. 7:16 And thine house and thy kingdom shall be established for ever before thee: thy throne shall be established for ever."

My principal, Dr. Eric Franks often preached on three things God says will abide forever. First, God abides forever. In Revelation 1: 8, John writes about the eternal nature of Jesus, "I am Alpha and Omega, the beginning and the ending, saith the Lord, which is, and which was, and which is to come, the Almighty." Secondly, God's Word abides forever (Ps 119:89) "For ever, O LORD, thy word is settled in heaven." Lastly, the person that does the will of God endures forever, "And the world passeth away, and the lust thereof: but he that doeth the will of God abideth for ever." How true a statement this is! I would like to add a Biblical principle. Everything God initiates lasts forever. He has the touch of eternity. Doesn't that give us a clue? The home is His work. We have proved God does have the "forever" quality. If the home is His design, it is designed to last forever. It must last a life time. It has the quality of durability. If we determine to establish it on God, it will last forever. The question is, are you willing to make that choice? This great institution God instituted can be built to last, but it all begins with a decision. It is a decision you and I must make. The decision is two-fold: first deciding to depend on God for salvation; then depending on God to build everything else in your life, especially the home.

Let me assure you, God wants us to build a home that lasts. He wants to have happy homes. He wants it to succeed. He wants the home to glorify Him. Will you say like Joshua, "And if it seem evil unto you to serve the LORD, choose you this day whom ye will serve; whether the gods which your fathers served that were on the other side of the flood, or the gods of the Amorites, in whose land ye dwell: but as for me and my house, we will serve the LORD." Will you build a home? Will you determine to invest in it? It is worth all the time, money, energy, and sacrifice you may make.

The foolish man built his house upon the sand, "And the rain descended, and the floods came, and the winds blew, and beat upon that house; and it fell: and great was the fall of it." Let us not be like the foolish man. Let us build on the "Rock," on the "Rock of Ages." A home built on the rock will stand strong.

God built the first home. He made Adam and Eve. They failed to follow His plan completely. He still chose to use them, love them and redeem them. Noah built the ark. In doing so, he served the Living God. Moses built the tabernacle. In doing so, he served the

Living God. Solomon built the temple. In doing so, he served Living God. Building the home is a serious task. God loves the home. He loves the family. He uses families to serve Him. He called Abraham to serve Him. In calling Abraham He called a family. Through the Bible you will find, God used so many families to fulfill His plans. So, build your home. Keep the family together. When you have built your home, you can serve God together as a family. It is easy to begin building a home, but a rather difficult task to complete it. Jesus came to earth to fulfill God's will. He served His father well. He lived a family life for thirty years. To the very end He took His responsibility seriously. He took good care of His mother to the very end. He was so committed to pleasing His heavenly Father. In John 4:34, "Jesus saith unto them, My meat is to do the will of him that sent me, and to finish his work." Let us have the same passion, the grit, and the nerve to build our homes. Let nothing stop us. We must not allow anything to tear it down. We must purpose to build a home that lasts. Let us build "the home." With God's help we can build a home that does not crumble. "WE CAN!" "WE CAN BUILD OUR HOME!"

END NOTES

CHAPTER ONE: I HAD A DREAM

1. M. A. Kribble, "Thomas Andrews The Builder of The Ship of Dreams" [journal on-line], available from http://www.geocities.com/athens/aegean/6136/; Internet; accessed 20 October 2008.

2. Ibid

3. "Titanic Statistics," [journal on-line], available from http://www.titanic-titanic.com/titanic-statistics.shtml; Internet; accessed 20 October 2008.

4. "How long did it take to build the Titanic?" QueryCat, 2007-2008 [journal on-line], available from http://www.querycat.com/faq/091414d2584be171a13ecdd742155a76; Internet; accessed 21 October 2008.

5. Ibid., M. A Kribble

6. Noelle Knox, "Dream house, sans spouse: more women buy homes," *USA TODAY*; [journal on-line], available from http://www.usatoday.com/money/2006-02-14-women-houses-usat_x.htm; Internet; accessed 21 October 2008.

7. Ibid.

8. Ibid.

9. "Most Expensive House In The World, Category"; *Property Investment Project 2008*; [journal on-line], available from http://www.propertyinvestmentproject.co.uk/blog/2007/03/09/most-expensive-house-in-the-world/; Internet; accessed 23 October 2008.

10. Ibid.

11. Jane Wells, "The World's Most Expensive House: A Whopping $500 Million!"11 July 2008; [journal on-line], available from http://www.cnbc.com/id/25642401; Internet; accessed 23 October 2008.

12. Home Sweet Home"; Poem hunter.com, 22 December 2008, [journal on-line], available from http://www.poemhunter.com/poem/home-sweet-home/; Internet; accessed 27 October 2008.

13. "Quotations Dare To Be Great!" Welcome to Quote Garden, 29 November 2008, [journal on-line], available from http://www.quotegarden.com/be-great.html; Internet; accessed 28 October 2008.

CHAPTER TWO: THE MASTER PLAN

1. "Future Forward Design For The World You Inhibit"; Inhabitat, 7 March 2007, [journal on-line]; available from http://www.inhabitat.com/2007/03/07/beijings-olympic-stadium-by-herzog-and-demeuron/; Internet; accessed 29 October 2008.

2. "Beijing National Stadium," Wikipedia, the free encyclopedia, [journal on-line]; available from http://en.wikipedia.org/wiki/Beijing_National_Stadium#Design_and_construction; Internet; accessed 29 October 2008.

3. Ibid.

4. Ibid.

5. "The Bible," Angelfire, 2001-2003, [journal on-line]; available from http://www.angelfire.com/my/HeartsPath/TheBible.html; Internet; accessed October 31 2008.

6. "Triangles and Arches in Architecture," Teachers' domain: WGBH Educational Foundation, 2002-2008 [journal on-line]; available from http://www.teachersdomain.org/resource/phy03.sci.phys.mfe.triarch/; Internet; accessed November 1 2008.

7. Stephen Caney, "Steven Caney's Ultimate Building Book" 2006; [journal on-line]; available from *http://books.google.com/books?id=AkfBLZzcI2gC&pg=PA205&lpg=PA205&dq=disney+Epcot+Center+dome&source=web&ots=nPVcgGG-k3&sig=PjEou1GfyKamVw1rXdt4bdCk7Qg&hl=en&sa=X&oi=book_result&resnum=3&ct=result#PPA206,M1*; Internet, accessed November 1 2008.

8. Haldor Lillenas; "The Bible Stands," [journal on-line]; available from, http://biblestudycharts.com/SH_The_Bible_Stands.html; Internet, accessed November 3 2008.

CHAPTER THREE: A MIGHTY FORTRESS

1. "Fortress," Merriam-Webster's online dictionary, [journal on-line]; available from http://www.merriam-webster.com/dictionary/fortress; Internet; accessed 4 November 2008.

2. Ibid., Stronghold.

3. "Great Wall of China," Wikipedia, the free encyclopedia; 22 December 2008; [journal on-line];available from http://en.wikipedia.org/wiki/Great_Wall_of_China; Internet; accessed 5 November 2008.

4. "A Mighty Fortress Is Our God," [journal on-line]; available from http://www.tanbible.com/tol_sng/amightyfortressisourgod.htm; Internet; accessed 10 November 2008.

5. Ibid.

6. Ibid.

CHAPTER FOUR: ROCK SOLID FOUNDATION

1. "Divorce Statistics - Divorce Rates," USALS, 2006, [journal on-line]; available from http://www.usattorneylegalservices.

com/divorce-statistics.html; Internet; accessed 18 November 2008.

2. Ibid.

3. Ibid.

4. Broken Family, "Statics," [journal on-line]; available from http://www.hisholychurch.net/net/broken.HTM; Internet; accessed 20 November 2008.

5. Ibid.

6. "Karthik Rajaram of Porter Ranch Kills Himself, Family," India Journal, 10 Oct. 2008, A1.

7. Ibid. A12.

CHAPTER FIVE: RAISING STRONG PILLARS: REMAINING IN GOD'S PRINCIPLES

1. Vine's Expository Dictionary of Biblical Words, PC Study Bible, Copyright (C) 1985, Thomas Nelson Publishers.

2. Ibid.

3. Swindoll, Charles R., Strike the Original Match, Multnomah press, Portland, Oregon, copyright 1980, pg 31.

4. "The Bible Stands," Lyrics and Composer: Haldor Lillenas, 1917, [journal on-line], available from http://biblestudycharts.com/SH_The_Bible_Stands.html; Internet; accessed 28 November 2008.

CHAPTER SIX: WEATHERING STROMS

1. "Storm," Wikipedia, the free encyclopedia; 2 December 2008; [journal on-line];available from http://en.wikipedia.org/wiki/Storm; Internet; accessed 22 November 2008.

2. Terry Lyles, *The Secret to Navigating Life's storms*, (Shippensburg: PA: Destiny Image Publishers, Inc: 2003), 21.

3. "Hurricane Katrina," Wikipedia, the free encyclopedia, 18 December 2008; [journal on-line], available from http://en.wikipedia.org/wiki/Hurricane_Katrina; Internet accessed on 27 November 2008.

4. Barbara Butler Norrell, *I'll Meet You At The Northeast Corner of Heaven*, (LARA Publishing: 2003), 86

5. Ibid.

6. Ibid.

7. "Personal Computer, Wikipedia, the free encyclopedia, 20 December 2008; [journal on-line]; available from http://en.wikipedia.org/wiki/Personal_computer; Internet accessed on 29 November 2008.

8. "Through It All", CHRISTIANLYRICSONLINE.COM. 2007; [journal on-line]; available from http://www.christianlyricsonline.com/artists/ray-boltz/through-it-all.html; Internet accessed on 29 November 2008.

CHAPTER SEVEN: CAUTION! WHAT ARE WE BUILDING? WHAT ARE WE LEAVING BEHIND?

1. "Memorizing the way to Heaven, Verse by Verse," The New York Times, 2006; [jounal on-line]; available from http://www.nytimes.com/2006/08/16/nyregion/16koran.html; Internet accessed on 30 November 2008.

2. Derry Brownfield, "Do your Children Study the Koran, 4 May 2008, [journal on–line]; available from http://www.newswith-

views.com/brownfield/brownfield65.htm; Internet accessed-on 31 November 2008.

3. Ibid

4. The Vine's Expository Dictionary of Biblical Words, PC study Bible, Copyright (C) 1985, Thomas Nelson Publishers)

CHAPTER EIGHT: THE LITTLE FOXES

1. "Elephants are Land Giants," Extreme Science; 1998-2002; [journal on-line] available from http://www.extremescience.com/AfricanElephant.htm; Internet accessed on 4 December 2008.

2. "Deadly Ants," Deccan Herald, 2007, [journal on-line]; available from http://www.deccanherald.com/CONTENT/Apr222008/environmet2008042163934.asp; Internet; accessed on 5 December 2007.

3. Ibid.

4. Ibid.

5. Ibid.

6. "Couple Spend Hundreds on Fox Bane; BBC NEWS; [journal on-line]; available from http://news.bbc.co.uk/2/hi/uk_news/england/london/5299616.stm; Internet; accessed on 5 December 2007.

7. Robert L. Phillips and Robert H. Schmidt, "Foxes" Internet Center For Wildlife Damage Management, 2005; [journal on-line]; available from http://icwdm.org/handbook/carnivor/Foxes.asp; Internet; accessed on 5 December 2008.

CHAPATER NINE:
EXCEPT THE LORD BUILD THE HOME

1. Adam Clarke Commentary, PC Study Bible Copyright (C) 1985, Thomas Nelson Publishers)

2. Dr. Roy Wallace, Lessons from the Tabernacle, (LinWel Ministries, Shreveport, Louisiana: LinWel Ministries: 2007), 5.

3. The Vine's Expository Dictionary of Biblical Words, PC Study Bible, Copyright (C) 1985, Thomas Nelson Publishers)

4. Ibid.

5. Adam Clarke Commentary, PC Study Bible, Copyright (C) 1985, Thomas Nelson Publishers)

6. Norell, Barbara Butler, Paula R. Bryant, *I'll Meet You at the Northeast Corner of Heaven*, (Lara publishing, 2003), xi.

7. "Paper Roses Lyrics, " MetroLyrics.com, 2004-2008, [journal on-line]; available from http://www.metrolyrics.com/paper-roses-lyrics-hank-snow.html; Internet; accessed on 10 December 2008.

8. Matthew Henry's Commentary, PC Study Bible, (Thomas Nelson Publishers: 1985).

9. Adam Clark's commentary, Power BibleCD, (Bronson, MI: Online Publishing Inc., 2000).

10. Ibid.

11. Ibid.

12. Ibid.

13. Dr. James Dobson, *Love Must Be Tough*, (Nashville: TN: Word Publishing: 1996) 38.

14. Adam Clark's Commentary, Power BibleCD, Bronson, MI: Online Publishing Inc., 2000).

15. Ibid.

16. "If That Isn't Love," KOVIDEO.NET, 1973, [journal on-line[available from http://www.kovideo.net/lyrics/e/Elvis-Presley/If-That-Isnt-Love.html; Internet, accessed on 10 December 2008.

CHAPTER TEN:
I COULDN'T HAVE DONE IT WITHOUT HIM

1. "Through It All Lyrics," Apostle, 16 September 2006, [journal on-line]; available from http://www.ap0s7le.com/list/song/2965/Ray_Boltz/Through_It_All/; Internet, accessed 15 December 2008.

2. "Amazing Grace," [journal on-line] available from http://www.tanbible.com/tol_sng/amazinggrace.htm; Internet, accessed on 15 December 2008.

3. Ibid.

4. "She Wears My Ring Lyrics by Johnny O'Keefe," Actionext, 2007-2008; [journal on-line]; available from; http://www.actionext.com/names_j/johnny_okeefe_lyrics/she_wears_my_ring.ht ml; Internet, accessed, 20 December 2008

CHAPTER ELEVEN: AS FOR ME AND MY HOME

1. Bruce E. Mills, *Help in Troubled Times,* (Los Angeles: The Judson Press, 1962), 80.

BIBLIOGRAPHY

"A Mighty Fortress Is Our God," [journal on-line]; available from http://www.tanbible.com/tol_sng/amightyfortressisourgod.htm; Internet; accessed 10 November 2008.

Adam Clarke Commentary, PC Study Bible, Copyright (C) 1985, Thomas Nelson Publishers)

"Amazing Grace," [journal on-line] available from http://www.tan-bible.com/tol_sng/amazinggrace.htm; Internet, accessed on 15 December 2008.

Broken Family, "Statics," [journal on-line]; available from http://www.hisholychurch.net/net/broken.HTM; Internet; accessed 20 November 2008.

"Beijing National Stadium," Wikipedia, the free encyclopedia, [journal on-line]; available from http://en.wikipedia.org/

wiki/Beijing_National_Stadium#Design_and_construction; Internet; accessed 29 October 2008.

Brownfield, Derry. "Do your Children Study the Koran, 4 May 2008, [journal on –line]; available from http://www.newswithviews.com/brownfield/brownfield65.htm; Internet accessed on 31 November 2008.

Caney, Stephen. "Steven Caney's Ultimate Building Book" 2006; [journal on-line]; available from http://books.google.com/books?id=AkfBLZzcI2gC&pg=PA205&lpg=PA205&dq=disney+Epcot+Center+dome&source=web&ots=nPVcgGG-k3&sig=PjEou1GfyKamVw1rXdt4bdCk7Qg&hl=en&sa=X&oi=book_result&resnum=3&ct=result#PPA206,M1; Internet, accessed November 1 2008.

"Couple Spend Hundreds on Fox Bane; BBC NEWS; [journal on-line]; available from http://news.bbc.co.uk/2/hi/uk_news/england/london/5299616.stm; Internet; accessed on 5 December 2007.

"Deadly Ants," Deccan Herald, 2007, [journal on-line]; available fromhttp://www.deccanherald.com/CONTENT/Apr222008/environmet2008042163934.asp; Internet; accessed on 5 December 2007.

"Divorce Statistics - Divorce Rates," USALS, 2006, [journal on-line]; available from http://www.usattorneylegalservices.com/divorce-statistics.html; Internet; accessed 18 November 2008.

Dobson, Dr. James. *Love Must Be Tough*, (Nashville: TN: Word Publishing: 1996) 38.

"Elephants are Land Giants," Extreme Science; 1998-2002; [journal on-line] available from http://www.extremescience.com/AfricanElephant.htm; Internet accessed on 4 December 2008.

"Future Forward Design For The World You Inhibit"; Inhabitat, 7 March 2007, [journal on-line]; available from http://www.inhabitat.com/2007/03/07/beijings-olympic-stadium-by-herzog-and-demeuron/; Internet; accessed 29 October 2008.

"Great Wall of China," Wikipedia, the free encyclopedia; 22 December 2008; [journal on-line];available from http://en.wikipedia.org/wiki/Great_Wall_of_China; Internet; accessed 5 November 2008.

"Hurricane Katrina," Wikipedia, the free encyclopedia, 18 December 2008; [journal on-line], available from http://en.wikipedia.

org/wiki/Hurricane_Katrina; Internet accessed on 27 November 2008.

"How long did it take to build the Titanic?" QueryCat, 2007-2008 [journal on-line], available from http://www.querycat.com/faq/091414d2584be171a13ecdd742155a76; Internet; accessed 21 October 2008.

"Home Sweet Home"; Poemhunter.com, 22 December 2008, [journal on-line], available from http://www.poemhunter.com/poem/home-sweet-home/; Internet; accessed 27 October 2008.

"If That Isn't Love," KOVIDEO.NET, 1973, [journal on-line] available from http://www.kovideo.net/lyrics/e/Elvis-Presley/If-That-Isnt-Love.html; Internet, accessed on 10 December 2008.

"Karthik Rajaram of Porter Ranch Kills Himself, Family," India Journal, 10 Oct. 2008, A1.India Journal, 10 Oct. 2008, A12.

Knox, Noelle. "Dream house, sans spouse: more women buy homes," *USA TODAY*; [journal on-line], available from http://www.usatoday.com/money/2006-02-14-women-houses-usat_x.htm; Internet; accessed 21 October 2008.

Kribble, M. A. "Thomas Andrews The Builder of The Ship of Dreams" [journal on-line], available from http://www.geocities.com/athens/aegean/6136/; Internet; accessed 20 October 2008.

Lillenas, Haldor. "The Bible Stands," [journal on-line]; available from, http://biblestudycharts.com/SH_The_Bible_Stands.html; Internet, accessed November 3 2008.

Lyles, Terry. *The Secret to Navigating Life's storms,* (Shippensburg: PA: Destiny Image Publishers, Inc: 2003), 21.

Matthew Henry's Commentary, PC Study Bible, (Thomas Nelson Publishers: 1985).

"Memorizing the way to Heaven, Verse by Verse," The New York Times, 2006; [jounal on-line]; available from http://www.nytimes.com/2006/08/16/nyregion/16koran.html; Internet accessed on 30 November 2008.

Merriam-Webster's online dictionary, "Fortress," [journal on-line]; available from http://www.merriam-webster.com/dictionary/fortress; Internet; accessed 4 November 2008.

….."Stronghold," [journal on-line]; available from http://www.merriam-webster.com/dictionary/fortress; Internet; accessed 4 November 2008.

Mills, Bruce E. Mills. *Help in Troubled Times,* (Los Angeles: The Judson Press, 1962), 80.

"Most Expensive House In The World, Category"; *Property Investment Project 2008*; [journal on-line], available from http://www.propertyinvestmentproject.co.uk/blog/2007/03/09/most-expensive-house-in-the-world/; Internet; accessed 23 October 2008.

Norell, Barbara Butler, Paula R. Bryant, *I'll Meet You at the Northeast Corner of Heaven*, (Lara publishing, 2003), xi.

…. *I'll Meet You At The Northeast Corner of Heaven,* (LARA Publishing: 2003), 86

"Paper Roses Lyrics, " MetroLyrics.com, 2004-2008, [journal on-line]; available from http://www.metrolyrics.com/paper-roses-lyrics-hank-snow.html; Internet; accessed on 10 December 2008.

"Personal Computer, Wikipedia, the free encyclopedia, 20 December 2008; [journal on-line]; available from http://en.wikipedia.org/wiki/Personal_computer; Internet accessed on 29 November 2008.

Phillips, Robert L. and Schmidt, Robert H. "Foxes" Internet Center For Wildlife Damage Management, 2005; [journal on-line]; available from http://icwdm.org/handbook/carnivor/Foxes.asp; Internet; accessed on 5 December 2008.

"Quotations Dare To Be Great!" Welcome to Quote Garden, 29 November 2008, [journal on-line], available from http://www.quotegarden.com/be-great.html; Internet; accessed 28 October 2008.

Robert L. Phillips and Robert H. Schmidt, "Foxes" Internet Center For Wildlife Damage Management, 2005; [journal on-line]; available from http://icwdm.org/handbook/carnivor/Foxes.asp; Internet; accessed on 5 December 2008.

"She Wears My Ring Lyrics by Johnny O'Keefe," Actionext, 2007-2008; [journal on-line]; available from; http://www.actionext.com/names_j/johnny_okeefe_lyrics/she_wears_my_ring.html; Internet, accessed, 20 December 2008

"Storm," Wikipedia, the free encyclopedia; 2 December 2008; [journal on-line];available from http://en.wikipedia.org/wiki/Storm; Internet; accessed 22 November 2008.

Swindoll, Charles R., Strike the Original Match, Multnomah press, Portland, Oregon, copyright 1980, pg 31.

"The Bible," Angelfire, 2001-2003, [journal on-line]; available from http://www.angelfire.com/my/HeartsPath/TheBible.html; Internet; accessed October 31 2008.

"The Bible Stands," Lyrics and Composer: Haldor Lillenas, 1917, [journal on-line], available from http://biblestudycharts.com/SH_The_Bible_Stands.html; Internet; accessed 28 November 2008.

"Through It All", CHRISTIANLYRICSONLINE.COM. 2007; [journal on-line]; available from http://www.christianlyricsonline.com/artists/ray-boltz/through-it-all.html; Internet accessed on 29 November 2008.

"Titanic Statistics," [journal on-line], available from http://www.titanic-titanic.com/titanic-statistics.shtml; Internet; accessed 20 October 2008.

"Triangles and Arches in Architecture," Teachers' domain: WGBH Educational Foundation, 2002-2008 [journal on –line]; available from http://www.teachersdomain.org/resource/phy03.sci.phys.mfe.triarch/; Internet; accessed November 1 2008.

The Vine's Expository Dictionary of Biblical Words, PC Study Bible, Copyright (C) 1985, Thomas Nelson Publishers.

Wallace, Dr. Roy. Lessons from the Tabernacle, (LinWel Ministries, Shreveport, Louisiana: LinWel Ministries: 2007), 5.

Wells, Jane. "The World's Most Expensive House: A Whopping $500 Million!"11 July 2008; [journal on-line], available from http://www.cnbc.com/id/25642401; Internet; accessed 23 October 2008.